Selenium IDE – A Practical Guide

Dr.C. Priya

Published by

Selenium IDE – A Practical Guide

ISBN 978-93-87862-63-0

Author
Dr.C. Priya
Bonfring
309, 2nd Floor,
5th Street Extension,
Gandhipuram, Coimbatore-641
012.
Tamilnadu, India.
E-mail: info@bonfring.org
Website: www.bonfring.org
Phone: 0422 4213231

Preface

Selenium is strong set of tools that is used for test automation. Selenium is a suite of tools that helps in automating web-based applications. This book will give an in-depth understanding of Selenium IDE and its related tools and their usage.

This book is designed for the streams such as BCA, B.Sc [IT], M.Sc [IT], MCA who would like to learn the basics of Selenium through practical examples. The book contains enough ingredients to get started with Selenium from where the students can take themselves to higher levels of expertise. Attempt has been made to present every concept in an easy way with simple programs. The programs/scripts are thoroughly checked and their results are displayed.

This book uses plain, lucid language to explain fundamentals of automation testing concepts. Selenium WebDriver is the most used automation tool for web-based applications. This book shows beginners how to create automated test cases using Selenium and will able to use Selenium IDE for quick throwaway test along with the automation framework development. I have provided prerequisites as well, so that the students are well versed with the topics needed to understand testing with Selenium IDE. This book provides logical method of explaining various complicated concepts and stepwise methods to explain the important topics. Data driven Testing using TestNG to create own automation framework. This book has been written for students at graduate level degree course in the Indian universities

This book contains 10 Chapters, each chapter is well supported with necessary illustrations and practical examples. All the chapters in this book are arranged in a proper sequence that permits each topic to build upon earlier studies. All care has been taken to make students comfortable in understanding the basic concept of testing. By the end of this book, the students will able to select any web application and automate it the way they want.

I invite readers, faculty members and students to offer their valuable comments and suggestions as feedback for further improvement of this book.

Dr.C. Priya

Acknowledgement

I express my deep gratitude to the creator, who created and nurture me in this transitory world.

I indebted my heartfelt gratitude to reverent Founder & Chancellor of Vels Institute of Science, Technology and Advanced Studies (VISTAS), Dr. Ishari K. Ganesh, M.Com., M.B.A., B.L., Ph.D., and Dr. Arthi K. Ganesh, Pro-Chancellor (Academic) for providing me conducive environment that helped me to author of this book today.

I express my highest tone of gratitude to Dr.A. Jothi Murugan, Vice-President of Vels Institute of Science, Technology and Advanced Studies (VISTAS), for giving me an opportunity to carry out the work through the esteemed institution

I express my indebtedness and gratitude to reverent Vice Chancellor Dr.P. Swaminathan for his scholarly guidance and valuable suggestions during the preparation of each chapter.

I wish to express my deep and sincere gratitude to Dr.A.R. Veeramani, Registrar for his guidance, support and persistent encouragement helped me to complete the book

I wish to extend my special thanks to Dr.P. Mayilvahanan, Director, School of Computing Sciences gave me lots of inputs and suggestions to bring out the best in me.

My hearfelt thanks to Dr.T. Kamalakannan, Head, Department of Information Technology, School of Computing Science for his extended valuable support that goes a long way for my academic progress.

I wish to thank all my colleagues as each one of them spent their valuable time encouraging me to do a valuable work.

I wish to thank the publishing professionals at Bonfring Publications for bringing out the book in its present form in record time.

Last but not least, I'm eternally grateful to my loving parents, husband and my amazing kids (R.P. Gurcharaen & R.P. Tharunika) for their love, understanding, prayers and continuing support to finish this book!

Dr.C. Priya

Author Profile

Dr.C. Priya, M.C.A., M.B.A., M.Phil(CS)., Ph.D.,

Dr.C. Priya received her Ph.D in Computer Applications from St.Peter's Institute of Higher Education and Research, Tamilnadu, India. She is currently working as Associate Professor, Department of Information Technology, School of Computing Sciences, Vels Institute of Science, Technology and Advanced Studies (VISTAS), Chennai, Tamilnadu, India. She has 11.6 years of teaching experience in Engineering, UG and PG level. Her research interest includes Cloud Computing, IoT, Block Chain Technology, Big Data Analytics, Machine Learning and Image Processing. She has produced one M.Phil research scholar and seven Ph.D scholars pursuing their research under her guidance.

She has received "Dr. A. P. J. Abdul Kalam Life Time Achievement National Award" from Innovative Research Developers and Publishers Awards October 2018. She has received "Excellence Teaching In Higher Education" from International Women Researchers Connect and Awards 2018 on Women's day and she has received "Best Teacher Award" on April 2009 at Saveetha Engineering College, India.

She has published 29 research papers in various International Journals such as Scopus and UGC referred journals. She serves as Editorial Board Member and Reviewer in various International Journals. She is an active member in Professional Bodies like Indian Society for Technical Education (ISTE) – Lifetime Membership, Computer Society of India (CSI), Indian Academic Researchers Association (IARA) - Lifetime Membership and Innovative Research Developers and Publishers (IRDP). She serves as Question Paper setter in various universities in Tamilnadu and Departmental Selection Committee Member for M.Phil and Ph.D Scholars at VISTAS.

CHAPTER 1

Introduction to Automation

1.1. Introduction

Automation testing is to automate the execution of manually designed test cases without any human intervention.

The purpose of automated testing is to execute manual functional tests quickly and in a cost-effective manner.

1.2. What is Functional Automation?

Frequently, we re-run tests that have been previously executed (also called regression testing) to validate functional correctness of the application.

Automation covers both,

Functional Automation: Used for automation of functional test cases in the regression test bed.

Performance Automation: Used for automation of non-functional performance test cases.

An example of this is measuring the response time of the application under considerable (for example 100 users) load.

Functional automation and performance automation are two distinct terms and their automation internals work using different driving concepts.

1.3. Why do we Automate?

- Effective Smoke (or Build Verification) Testing
- Standalone - Lights Out Testing
- Increased Repeatability
- Testers can Focus on Advanced Issues
- Higher Functional Test Coverage

1.4. Key benefits of Functional Automation

Reliable: Tests perform precisely the same operations each time they are run, thereby eliminating human error.

Repeatable: You can test how the software reacts under the repeated execution of the same operations.

Programmable: You can program sophisticated tests that bring out hidden information from the application.

Comprehensive: You can build a suite of tests that cover every feature in your application.

Reusable: You can re-use tests on different versions of an application, even if the user-interface changes.

Better Quality Software: Because you can run more tests in less time with fewer resources.

Fast: Automated tools run tests significantly faster than human users.

1.5. Economics of Automation

Calculating the **Cost of Test Automation**

Cost of Automation = Cost of tool + labor cost of script creation +labor cost of script maintenance

Automate if

Cost of automation *is lower than the manual execution of those scripts.*

1.6. Commercial and Open Source Automation Tools

This section lists some of the popular Commercial and Open Source Automation Tools.

Vendor	Tool	Details
OpenSource (free)	Selenium	Open Source tools and market leader in the Open Source segment. Primary for WWeb-based automation. Support C#, Java, Python, and Ruby as programming language.
OpenSource (free)	Watir	Watir stands for "Web application testing in Ruby". It is again primarily for WWeb application automation and uses Ruby as the programming language.
HP	Unified Functional Testing	HP UFT (previous version was called QTP) is the market leader in Test Automation in the commercial tools segment. It uses VBScript as the programming language and its ease of use makes it a tool of choice against other competing tools.
IBM	Rational Functional Tester	IBM Rational Functional tester is another popular test Automation Tool. We can program in VB.net or Java using this tool. Is recommended for technical testers.
Microfocus	SilkTest	Microfocus bought SilkTest from Borland. It is still a very popular automation tool which uses 4Test (propriety) language. Good for technical testers.
Microsoft	VSTP – Coded UI tests	Coded UI tests come with Microsoft Visual studio Ultimate or Premium version. You can program using VB.net or C# as languages of choice. Fairly good for technical testers.
SmartBear	TestComplete	Low cost alternative to other commercial tools with good features for automation. You have the option to program using VBScript, JScript, C++Script, C#Script or DelphiScript language.

CHAPTER 2

Introduction to Selenium

2.1. History of Selenium

- Selenium was **created by Jason Huggins in 2004**.

- The Original name is JavaScript Functional Tester [JSFT]

- Open source browser based integration test framework built originally by Thoughtworks.

- 100% JavaScript and HTML

- Web testing tool

- Supports testing Web 2.0 applications

- Supports for Cross-Browser Testing(on Multiple Browsers)

- Multiple Operating Systems

- Cross browser – IE 6/7, Firefox .8+, Opera, Safari 2.0+

2.2. What is Selenium?

- Selenium is a free (open source) automated testing suite for web applications across different browsers and platforms.

- It is quite similar to HP Quick Test Pro (QTP now UFT- Unified Functional Testing) only that Selenium focuses on automating web-based applications.

- Testing done using Selenium tool is usually referred as Selenium Testing.

- Selenium is not just a single tool, but a suite of software's, each catering to different testing needs of an organization.

2.3. Selenium Components

It has four components.

- Selenium Integrated Development Environment (IDE)

- Selenium Remote Control (RC)

- WebDriver

- Selenium Grid

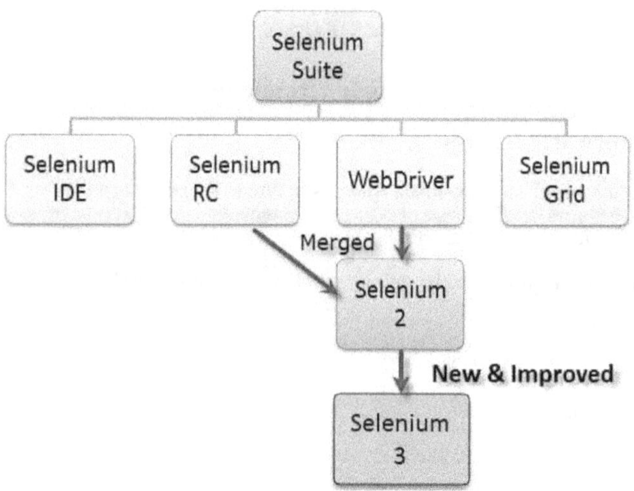

At the moment, Selenium RC and WebDriver are merged into a single framework to form **Selenium 2.** Selenium 1, by the way, refers to Selenium RC.

2.4.   So, Why the Name Selenium?

It came from a joke which Jason cracked one time to his team. Another automated testing framework was popular during Selenium's development, and it was by the company called **Mercury Interactive** (yes, the company who originally made QTP before it was acquired by HP). Since Selenium is a well-known antidote for Mercury poisoning, Jason suggested that name. His teammates took it, and so that is how we got to call this framework up to the present.

2.5. Selenium IDE

- Shinya Kasatani of Japan created Selenium IDE, a Firefox extension that can automate the browser through a record-and-playback feature.
- Selenium IDE (Integrated Development Environment) is the simplest framework in the Selenium suite and is the easiest one to learn.
- It is a Firefox plugin that you can install as easily as you can with other plugins.
- It is effortless to install and easy to learn.
- Selenium IDE should only be used as a prototyping tool
- To use Selenium IDE without prior knowledge in programming, you should at least be familiar with HTML, JavaScript, and the DOM (Document Object Model) to utilize this tool to its full potential.
- Knowledge of JavaScript will be required when we get to the section about the Selenese command "runScript."
- Selenium IDE supports auto complete mode when creating tests.

This feature serves two purposes:

- It helps the tester to enter commands more quickly.
- It restricts the user from entering invalid commands.

2.6. PROS and CONS of Selenium IDE

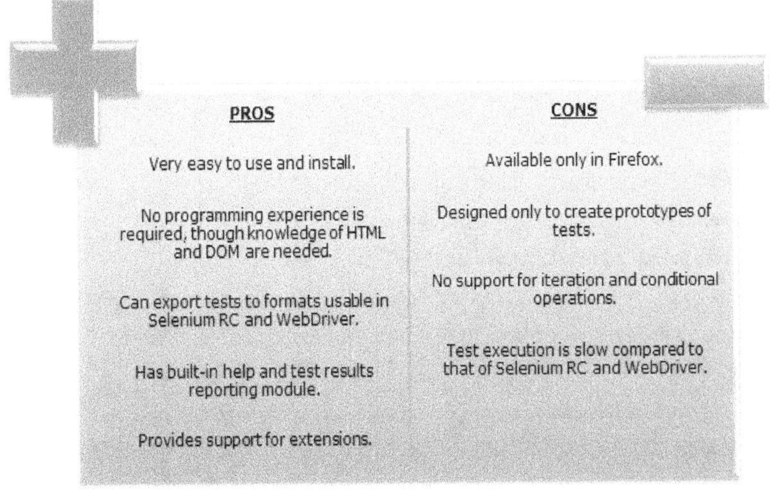

2.7. Features of Selenium IDE

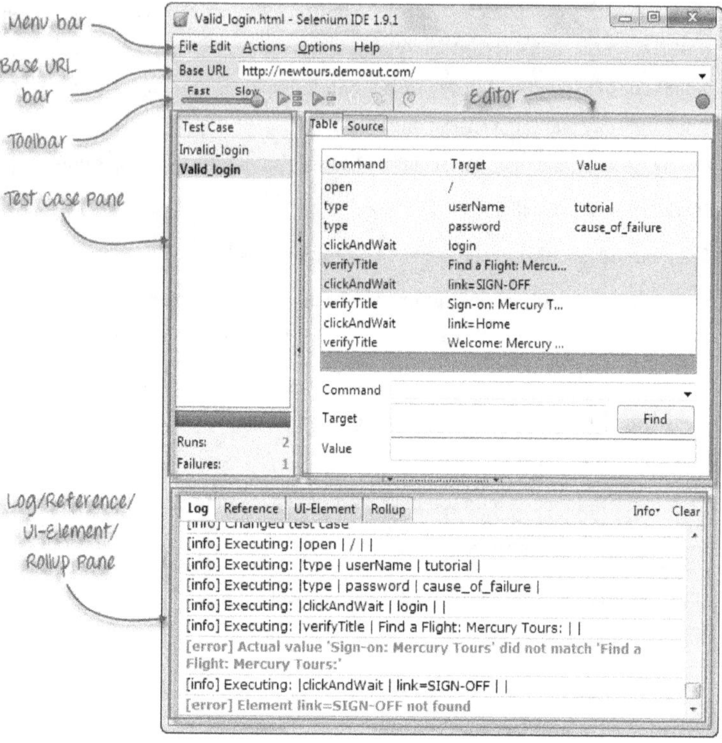

2.8. Menu Bar

It is located at the **topmost portion** of the IDE. The most commonly used menus are the File, Edit, and Options menus.

2.8.1. File Menu

- It contains options to create, open, save and close tests.
- Tests are **saved in HTML format**.
- The most useful option is **"Export"** because **it allows you to turn your Selenium IDE test cases into file formats that can run on Selenium Remote Control and WebDriver**
- **"Export Test Case As..."** will export only the current opened test case.
- **"Export Test Suite As..."** will export all the test cases in the currently opened test suite.

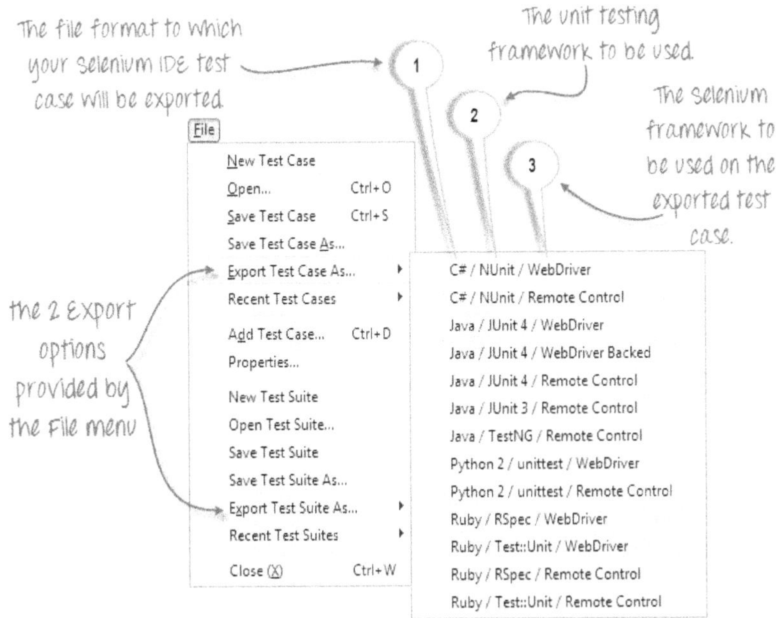

As of **Selenium IDE v1.9.1**, test cases can be exported only to the following formats:

- .cs (C# source code)
- .java (Java source code)
- .py (Python source code)
- .rb (Ruby source code)

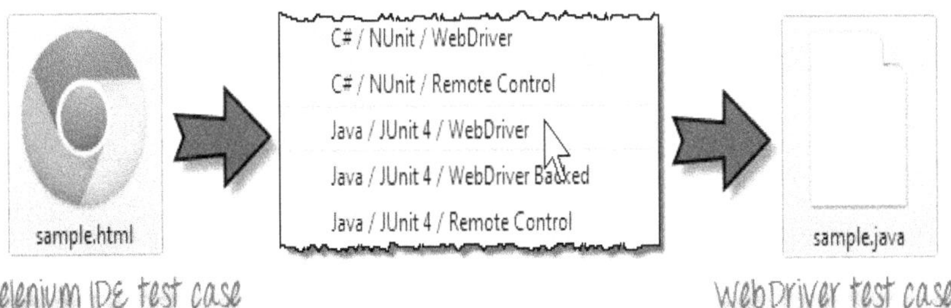

2.8.2. Edit Menu

- It contains the usual options like Undo, Redo, Cut, Copy, Paste, Delete, and Select All.
- The two most important options are the "**Insert New Command**" and "**Insert New Comment**".

- The newly inserted command or comment will be placed on top of the current selected line.

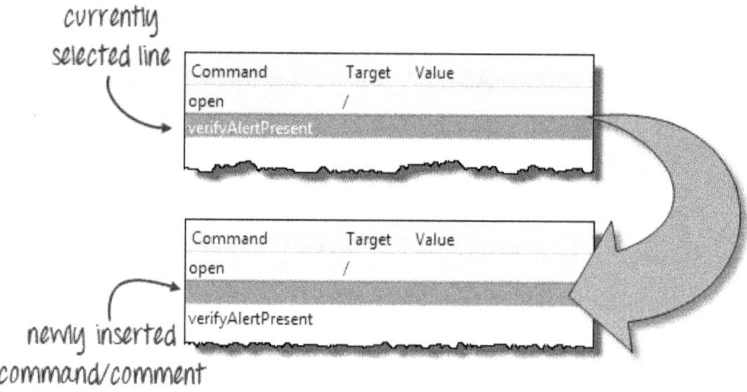

- Commands are colored black.
- Comments are colored purple.

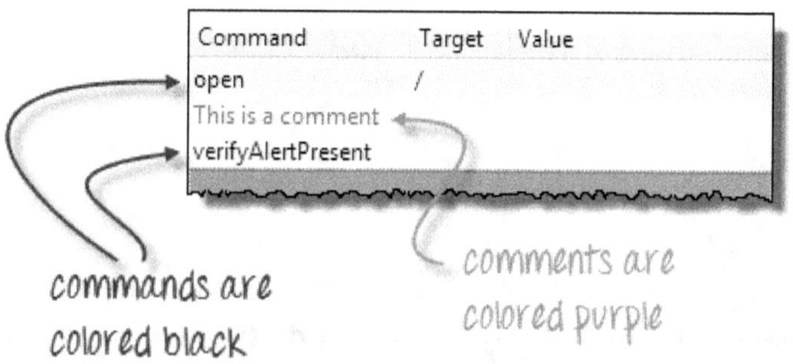

2.8.3. Options Menu

It provides the **interface for configuring various settings** of Selenium IDE.

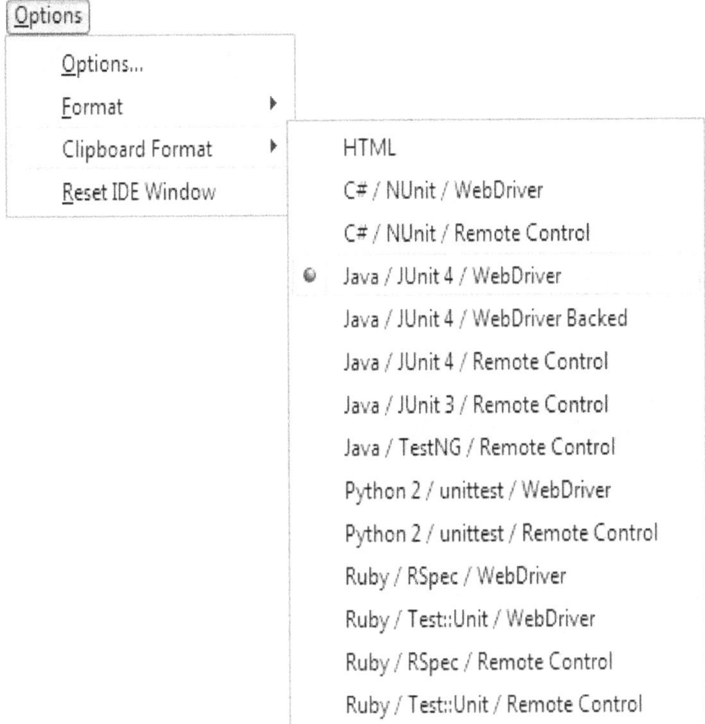

2.9.   Clipboard Format

The Clipboard Format allows you to copy a Selenese command from the editor and paste it as a code snippet.

- The format of the code follows the option you selected here in Clipboard Format's list. **HTML** is **the default selection.**

For example, when you choose **Java/JUnit 4/WebDriver** as your clipboard format, every Selenese command you copy from Selenium IDE's editor will be pasted as **Java code**.

2.10. Selenium IDE Options Dialog Box

The Selenium IDE Options dialog box by clicking Options > Options... on the menu bar. Though there are many settings available, we will concentrate on the few important ones.

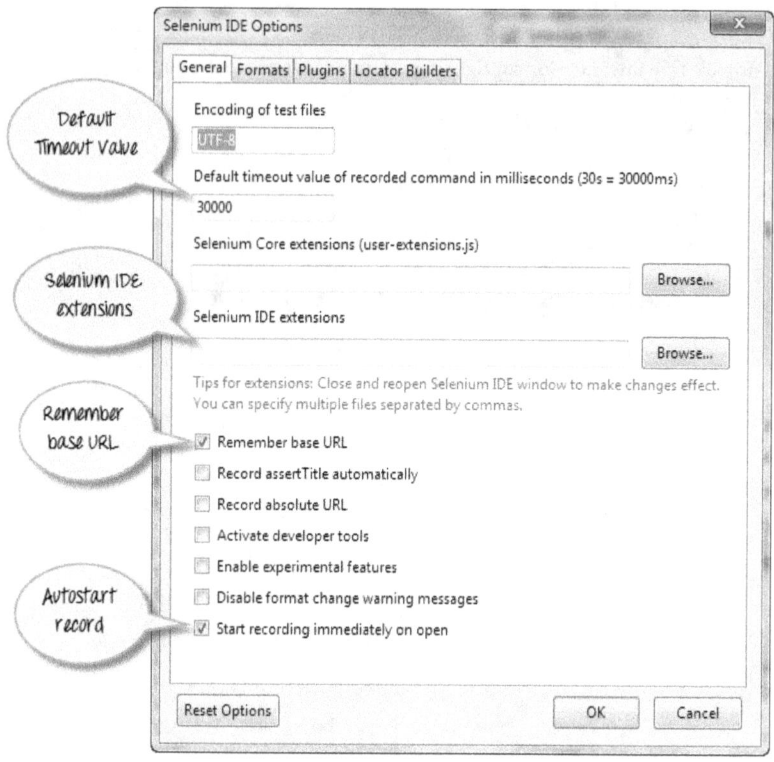

- **Default Timeout Value**. This refers to the time that Selenium has to wait for a certain element to appear or become accessible before it generates an error. The **Default timeout value is 30000ms**.

- **Selenium IDE extensions**. To extend Selenium IDE's capabilities and use "Selenium" as a keyword to search for the specific extensions.

- **Remember base URL.** Keep this checked if you want Selenium IDE to remember the Base URL every time you launch it.

- **Autostart record.** If you check this, Selenium IDE will immediately record your browser actions upon startup.

- **Locator builders.** Locators are generated while recording. **Locators are ways to tell Selenium IDE which UI element should a Selenese command act upon.**

- In the setup below, when you click on an element with an ID attribute, that element's ID will be used as the locator since "id" is the first one in the list. The list goes on and on until an appropriate one is found.

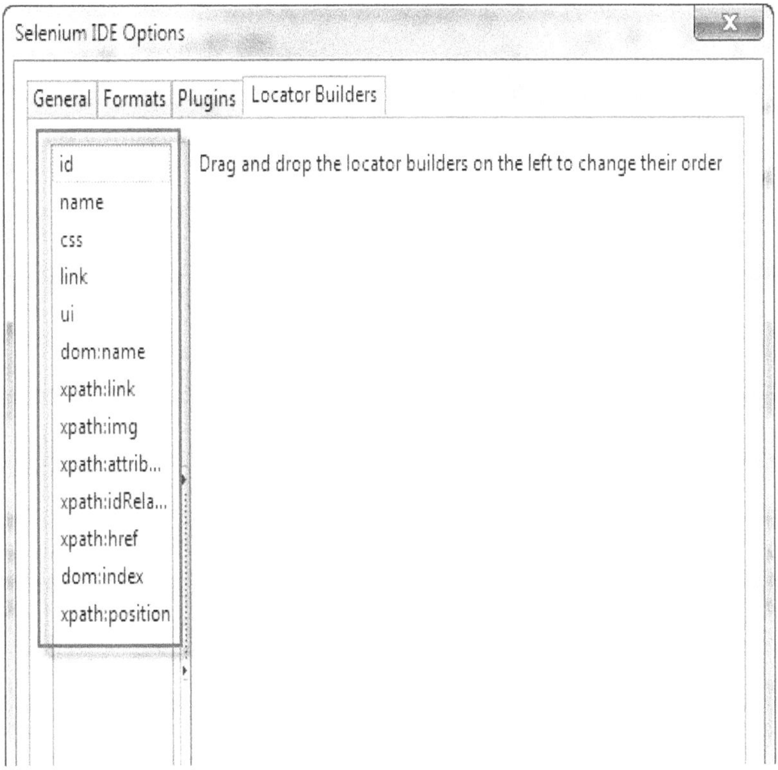

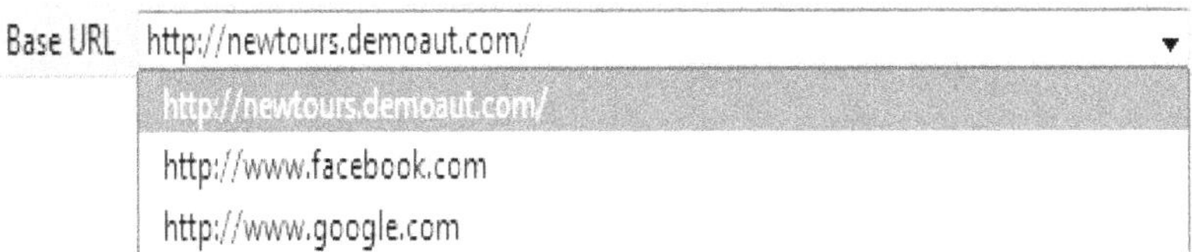

2.11. Base URL Bar

- It has **a** dropdown **menu that remembers all previous values** for easy access.

- The Selenese command **"open" will take you to the URL that you specified in the Base URL**.

- **The Base URL** is **very useful in accessing relative URLs**. Suppose that your Base URL is set to http://newtours.demoaut.com. When you execute the command "open" with the target value "signup," Selenium IDE will direct the browser to the sign-up page. See the illustration below.

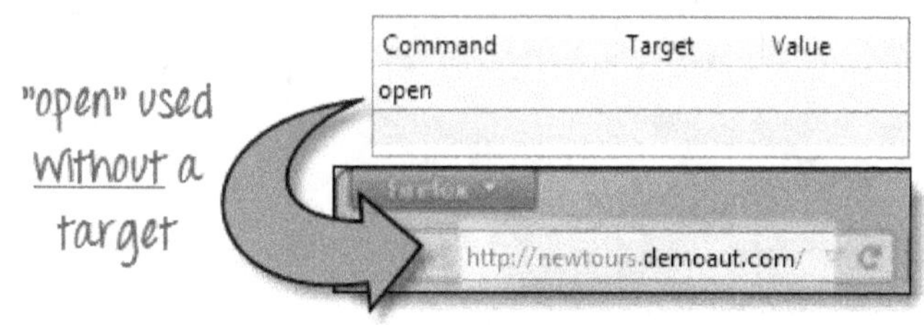

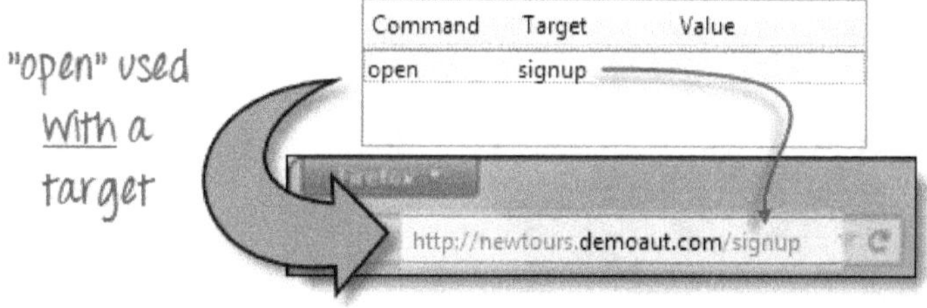

2.12. Toolbar

Fast — Slow	**Playback Speed**. This controls the speed of your Test Script Execution.
●	**Record.** This starts/ends your recording session. Each browser action is entered as a Selenese command in the Editor.
▷▤	**Play entire test suite**. This will sequentially play all the test cases listed in the Test Case Pane.
▷▬	**Play current test case**. This will play only the currently selected test case in the Test Case Pane.
◁▷	**Pause/Resume**. This will pause or resume your playback.
⤵	**Step**. This button will allow you to step into each command in your test script.
↻	**Apply rollup rules**. This is an advanced functionality. It allows you to group Selenese commands together and execute them as a single action.

2.13. Test Case Pane

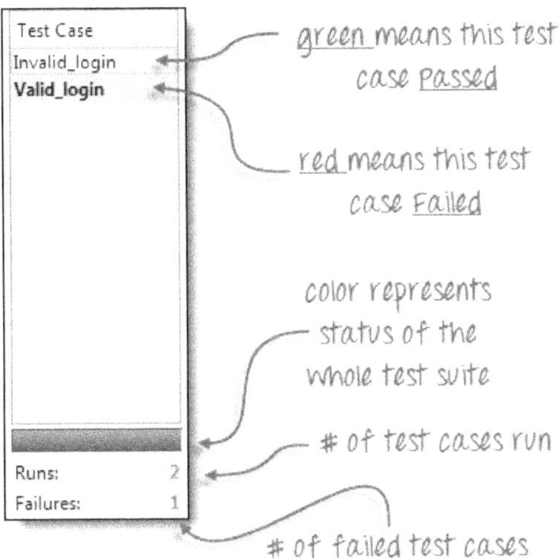

- In Selenium IDE, you can open **more than one test case at a time**.
- **The test case pane shows you the list of currently opened test cases.**
- When you open a test suite, the test case pane will **automatically list all the test cases** contained in it.
- The test case written in **bold font** is the **currently selected test case**
- After playback, **each test case is color-coded** to represent if it passed or failed.
  - Green color means "Passed."
  - Red color means "Failed."
- At the bottom portion is a summary of the number of test cases that were run and failed.

2.14. Editor

You can think of the editor as **the place where all the action happens**. It is available in two views: Table and Source.

Table View

- Most of the time, you will work on Selenium IDE using the **Table View**.
- This is **where you create and modify Selenese commands.**
- After playback, each step is color-coded.

- To create steps, type the name of the command in the "Command" text box.
- It displays **a** dropdown list of commands that match with the entry that you are currently typing.
- Target is any parameter (like username, password) for a command and
- Value is the input value (like tom, 123pass) for those Targets.

2.15. Source View

- It displays the steps in HTML (default) format.
- It also allows you to edit your script just like in the Table View.

```
<tr>
        <td>verifyTitle</td>
        <td>Sign-on: Mercury Tours </td>
        <td></td>
</tr>
<tr>
        <td>clickAndWait</td>
        <td>link=Home</td>
        <td></td>
</tr>
<tr>
        <td>verifyTitle</td>
        <td>Welcome: Mercury Tours</td>
        <td></td>
</tr>
</tbody></table>
</body>
</html>
```

2.16. Log Pane

The Log Pane displays runtime messages during execution. It provides real-time updates as to what Selenium IDE is doing.

Logs are Categorized Into Four Types

1. Debug   - By default, Debug messages are not displayed in the log panel
2. Info   - It says which command Selenium IDE is currently executing
3. Warn   - These are warning messages that are encountered in special situations
4. Error   - These are error messages generated when Selenium IDE fails to execute a command

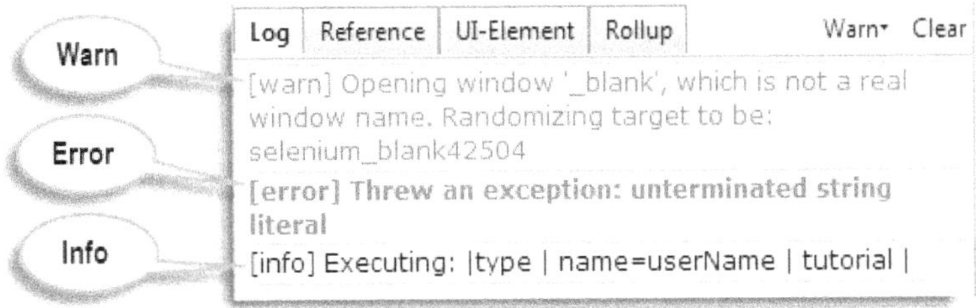

Logs can be filtered by type. For example, if you choose to select the "Error" option from the dropdown list, the Log Pane will show error messages only.

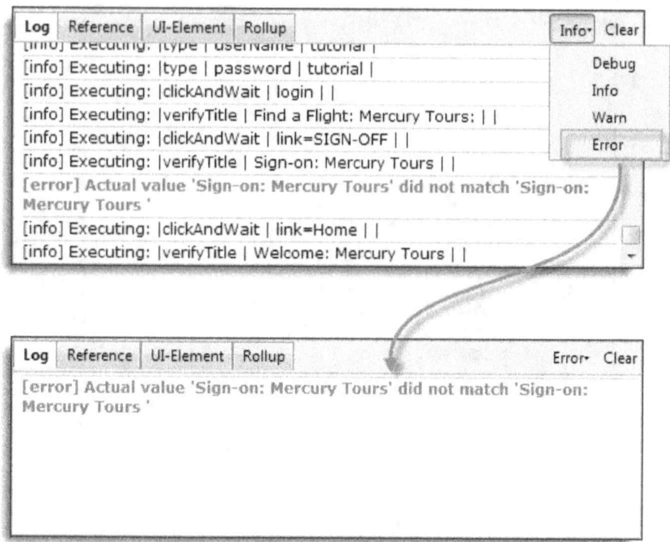

2.17. Reference Pane

- **The Reference Pane shows a concise description of the currently selected Selenese command in the Editor.**

- It also shows the **description about the locator and value** to be used in that command.

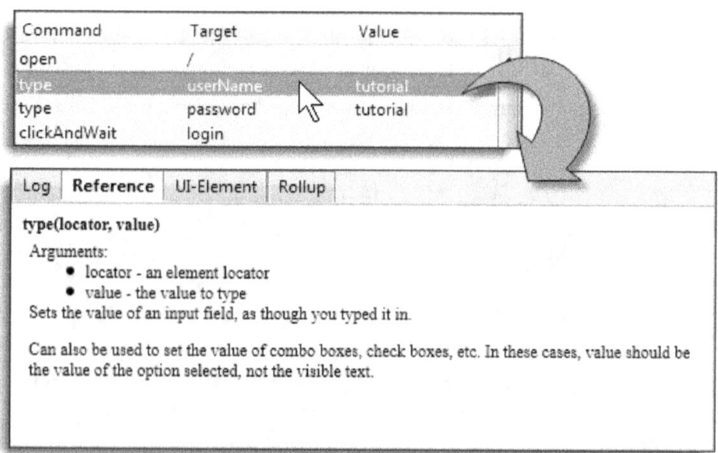

2.18. UI-Element Pane

The UI-Element is for advanced Selenium users.

- It uses JavaScript Object Notation (JSON) to define element mappings.
- The documentation and resources are found in the "UI Element Documentation" option under the Help menu of Selenium IDE.

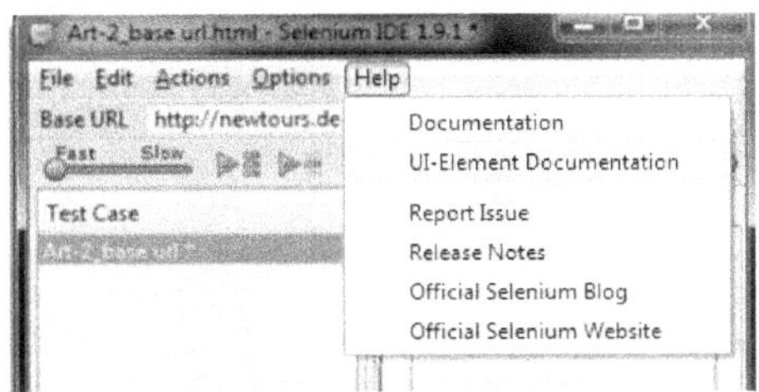

An example of a UI-element screen is shown below.

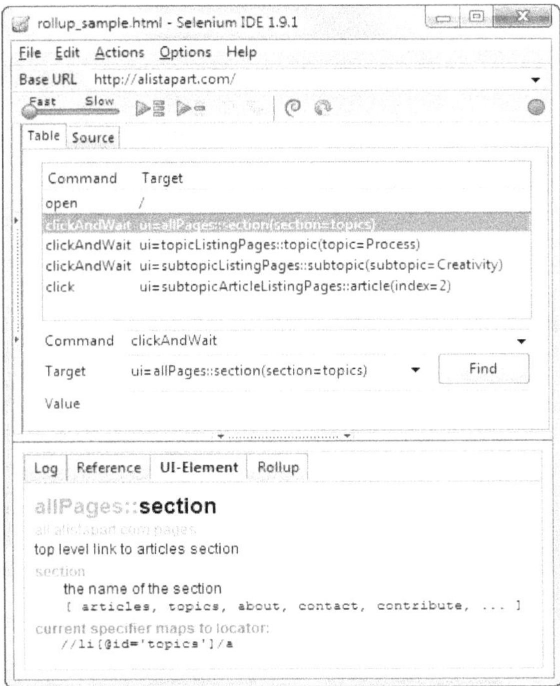

2.19. Rollup Pane

Rollup allows you to execute a group of commands in one step. A group of commands is simply called as a "rollup." It employs heavy use of JavaScript and UI-Element concepts to formulate a collection of commands that is similar to a "function" in programming languages.

Rollups are reusable; meaning, they can be used multiple times within the test case. Since rollups are groups of commands condensed into one, they contribute a lot in shortening your test script.

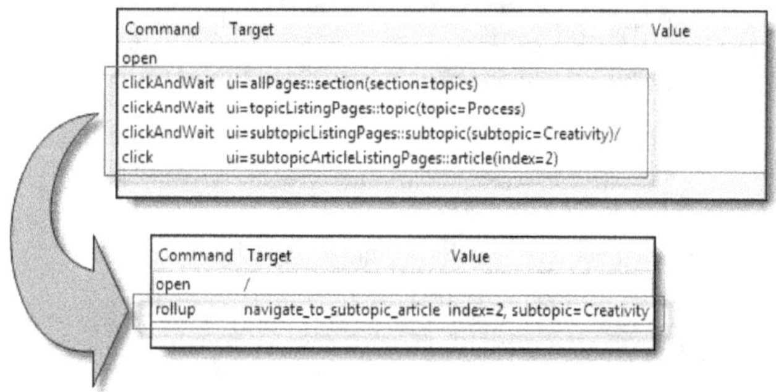

An example of how the contents of the rollup tab look like is shown below.

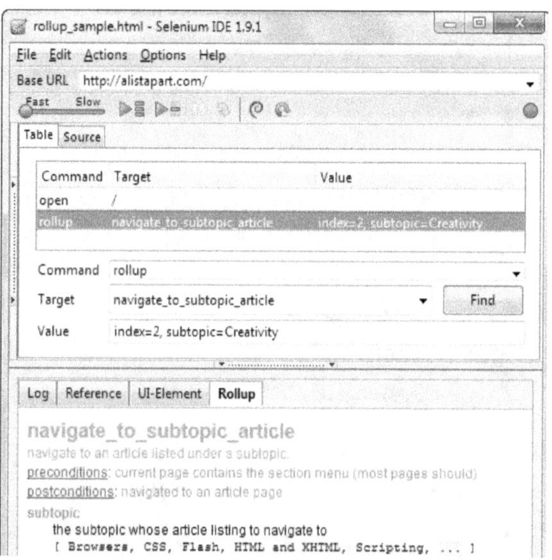

CHAPTER 3

Installing Selenium Components

3.1.   Installing Selenium IDE

Pre-requisite – Mozilla Firefox browser should be installed locally on the test machine.

1. Launch Mozilla FireFox browser and open URL http://seleniumhq.org/download/ to download Selenium IDE from the SeleniumHQ download Page.

2. Click on Selenium - Web Browser Automation.

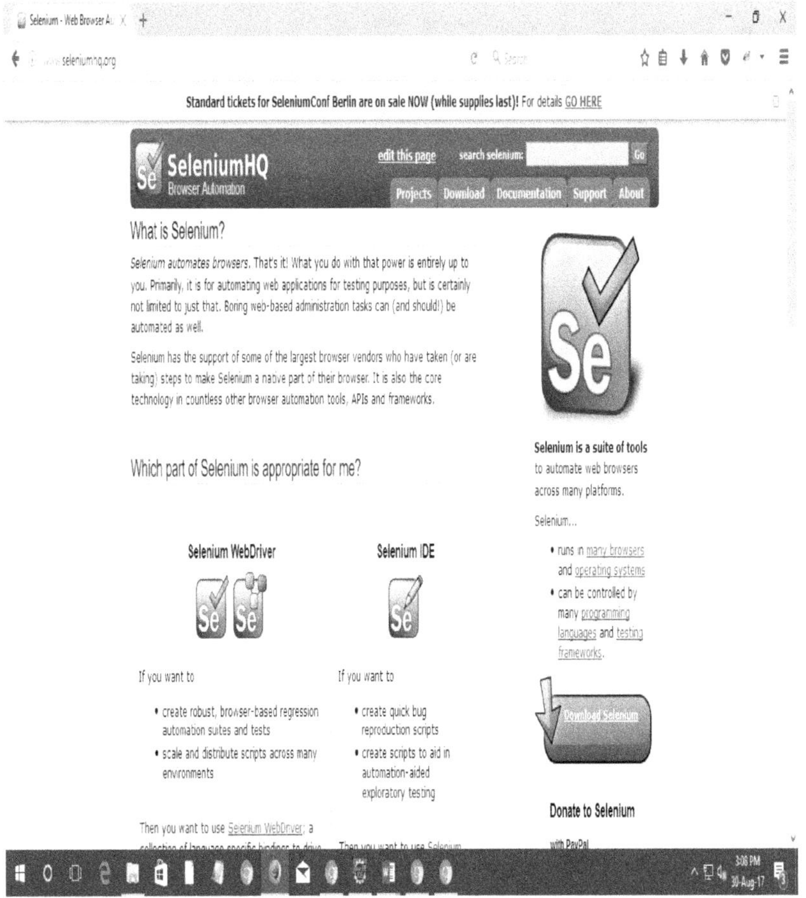

1. **Click Download Selenium**

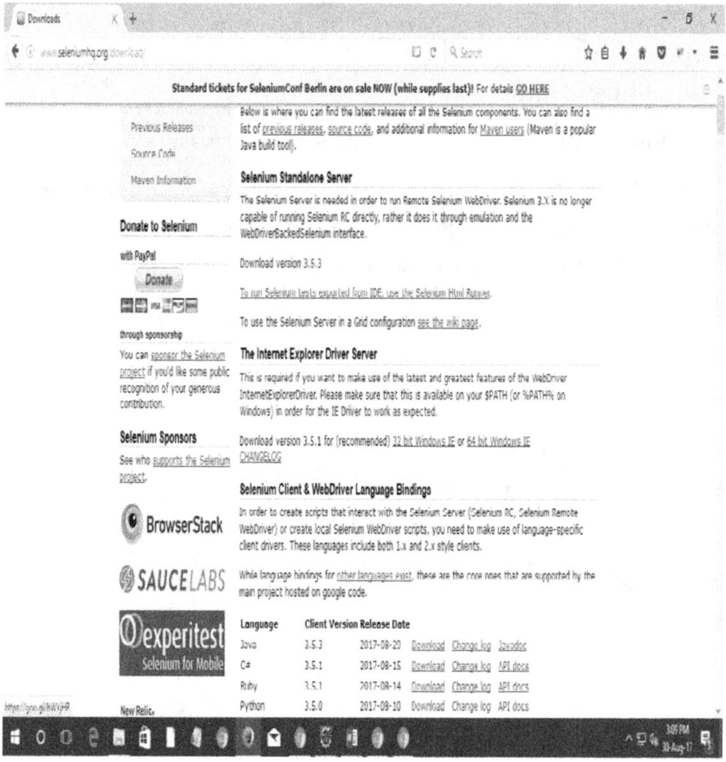

2. **Click to download version 3.5.3**

    Tools → Selenium IDE

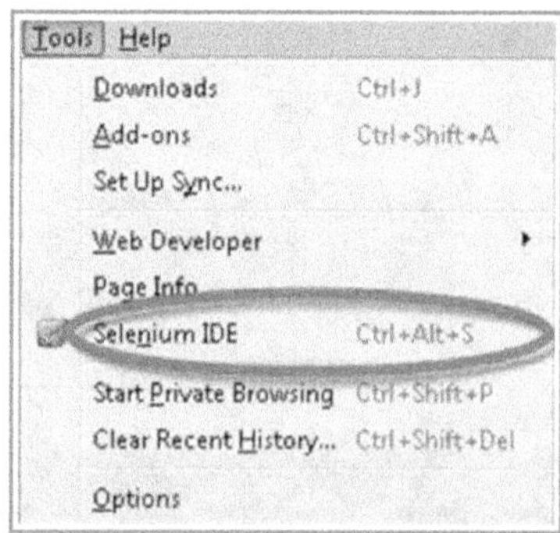

After Firefox reboots you will find the Selenium-IDE listed under the Firefox Tools menu. Go to

3. Click from addons.mozilla.org

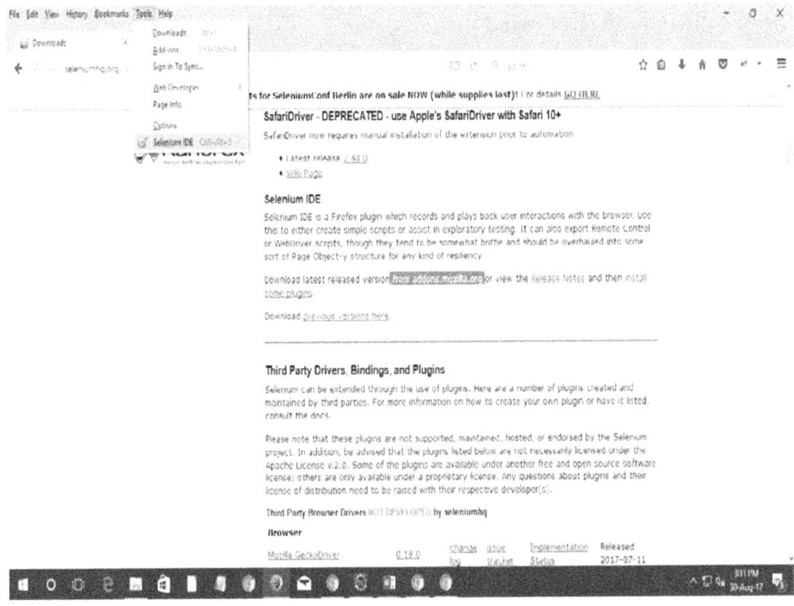

4. Check Selenium IDE is added in Tools menu

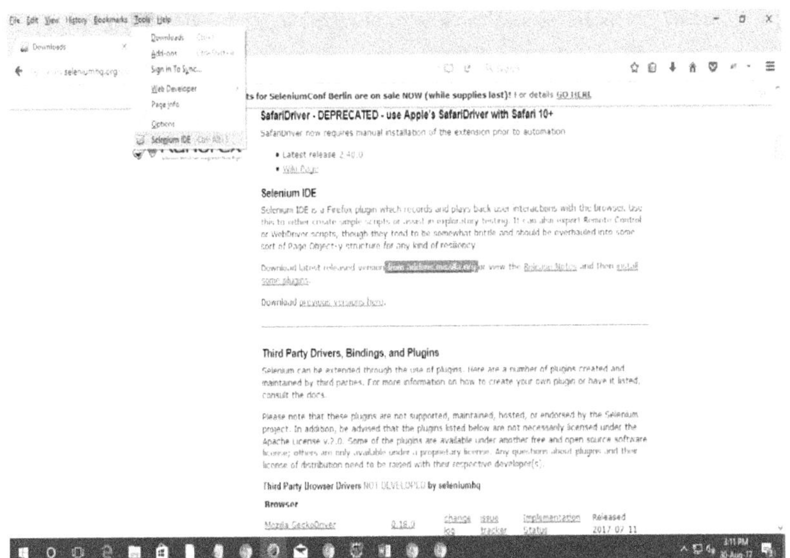

3.2.   Installing Firebug Plug-In

- Install Firefox add-on Firebug

- Firebug integrates with Firefox to give access to Web development tools to edit, debug, and monitor CSS, HTML, and JavaScript live in any Web page.

- In Selenium, **Firebug helps in inspecting UI elements** and finding its associated properties and values.

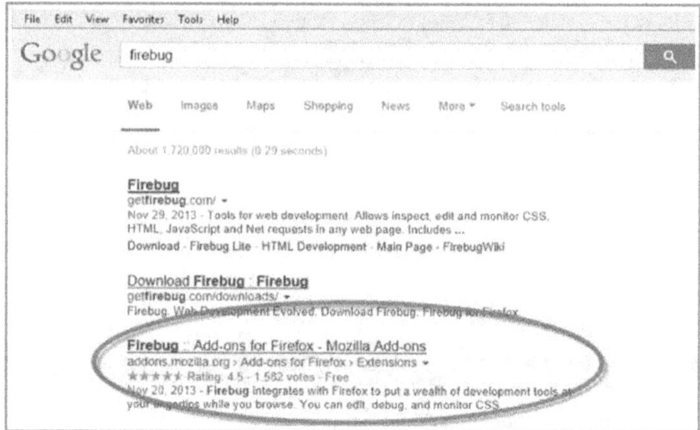

1. To install Firebug add-ons, Open Firefox browser, launch www.google.com and search for Firebug. Click on Firebug link.

2. Add-ons page appears. Click on + Add to Firefox button.

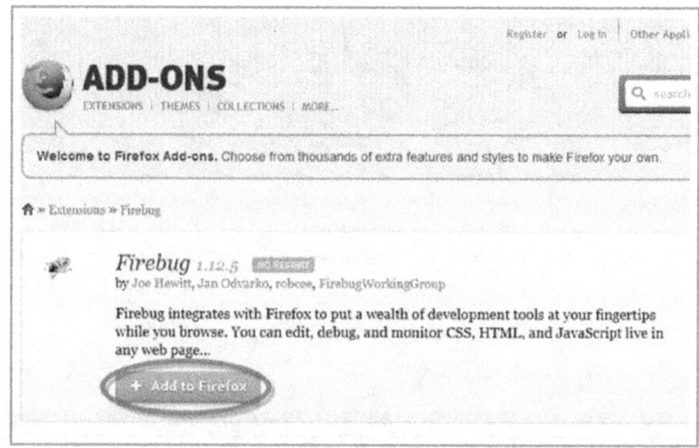

3. Wait for Firebug add-ons to be downloaded. Once downloaded, click on Install Now button in the Software Installation pop-up.

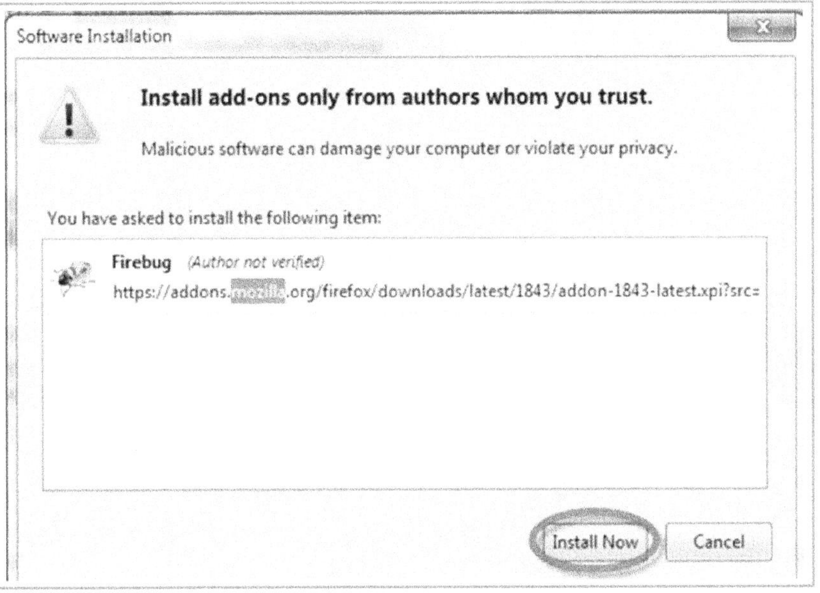

CHAPTER 4

Introducing Selenium Commands

4.1.   Selenium Commands

- The command set is often called Selenese.
- Selenium commands come in three "flavors":
  - Actions
  - Accessory and
  - Assertions.

Actions

- User actions on application / Command the browser to do something.
- Actions are commands that generally manipulate the state of the application.
- Click link- click / Clickandwait.

Accessory

Accessory examine the state of the application and store the results in variables, e.g. "storeTitle".

Assertions

For validating the application we are using Assertions

- For verifying the web pages
- For verifying the text
- For verifying alerts

Assertions can be used in 3 modes:

- assert
- verify
- waitFor

Example: "assertText","verifyText" and "waitForText".

Note

- When an "assert" fails, the test is aborted.
- When a "verify" fails, the test will continue execution.
- "waitFor"commandswaitforsomeconditiontobecometrue.

4.2. Commonly Used Selenium Commands

These are probably the most commonly used commands for building test.

Command	Description
Open	Opens a page using a URL
click/clickAndWait	Performs a click operation, and optionally waits for a new page to load.
verifyTitle/assertTitle	Verifies an expected page title
verifyTextPresent	Verifies expected text is somewhere on the page.
verifyElementPresent	Verifies an expected UI element, as defined by its HTML tag, is present on the page.
verifyText	Verifies expected text and it's corresponding HTML tag are present on the page.
verifyTable	Verifies a table's expected contents.
waitForPageToLoad	Pauses execution until an expected new page load. Called automatically when clickAndWait is used
waitForElementPresent	Pauses execution until an expected UI element, as defined by its HTML tag, is present on the page

4.3. Recording and Run Settings

- When Selenium-IDE is first opened, the record button is **ON by default**.
- During recording, Selenium-IDE will automatically insert commands into your test case based on youractions.

Remember Base URL MODE - Using Base URL to Run Test Cases in Different Domains

Record Absolute recording mode – Run Test Cases in Particular Domain.

4.4. Running Test Cases

Run a Test Case

Click the Run button to run the currently displayed test case.

Run a Test Suite

Click the Run All button to run all the test cases in the currently loaded test suite.

Stop and Start

- The Pause button can be used to stop the test case while it is running.
- The icon of this button then changes to indicate the Resume button.
- To continue click Resume.

Stop in the Middle

- You can set a breakpoint in the test case to cause it to stop on a particular command.
- This is useful for debugging your test case.
- To set a breakpoint, select a command, right-click, and
- From the context menu select Toggle Breakpoint.

Start from the Middle

- You can tell the IDE to begin running from a specific command in the middle of the test case.
- This also is used for debugging.
- To set a start point, select a command, right-click, and
- From the context menu select Set/Clear Start Point.

Run Any Single

- Command Double-click any single command to run it by itself.
- This is useful when writing a single command.
- It lets you immediately test a command you are constructing, when you are not sure if it is correct.
- You can double-click it to see if it runs correctly.
- This is also available from the context menu.

4.5. Test Suite

- A test suite is a collection of tests. Often one will run all the tests in a test suite as one continuous batch-job.
- When using Selenium-IDE, test suites also can be defined using a simple HTML file
- The syntax again is simple. An HTML table defines a list of tests where each row defines the file system path to each test.

CHAPTER 5

Creating First Selenium IDE Script

5.1.   Creating Selenium IDE Tests

The following steps are involved in creating Selenium tests using IDE:

- Recording and adding commands in a test
- Saving the recorded test
- Saving the test suite
- Executing the recorded test

5.1.1. Recording and Adding Commands in a Test

Use URL **www.ncalculators.com** to demonstrate the features of Selenium.

Step 1 : Launch the Firefox browser and navigate to the website:
http://www.ncalculators.com/

Step 2 : Open Selenium IDE from the Tools menu and press the record button that is on the top-right corner.

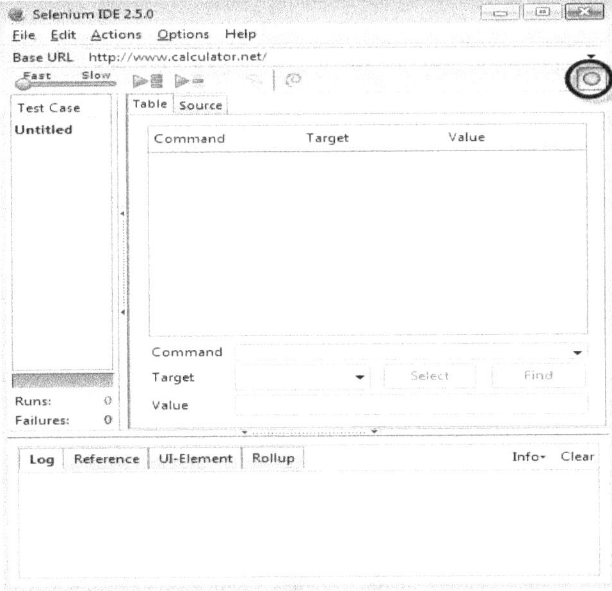

Step 3 : Navigate to "Math Calculator" >> "Percent Calculator >> enter "10" as number1 and 50 as number 2 and click "calculate".

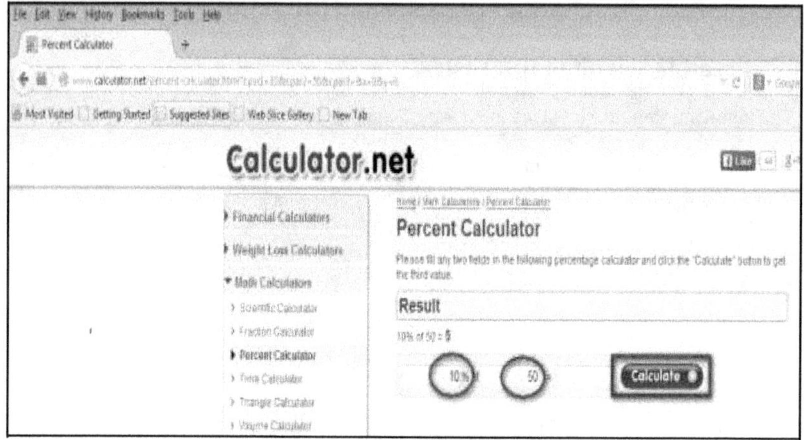

Step 4 : User can then insert a checkpoint by right clicking on the web element and select "Show all available commands" >> select "assert text css=b 5"

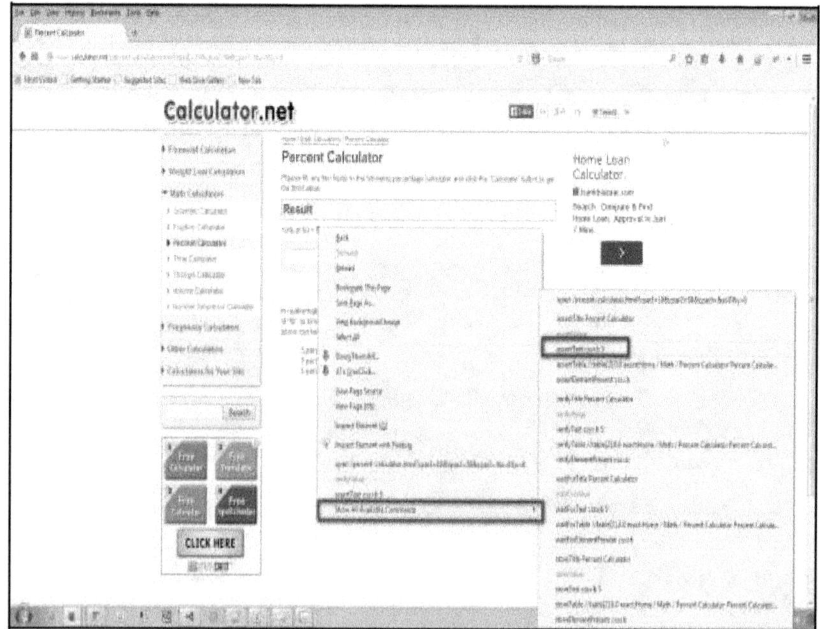

Step 5 : The recorded script is generated and the script is displayed as shown below.

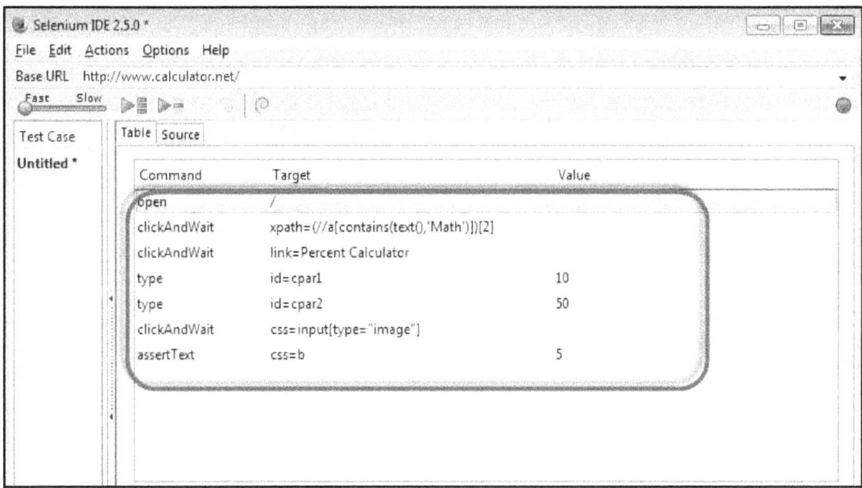

5.1.2. Saving the Recorded Test

Step 1 : Save the Test Case by navigating to "File" >> "Save Test" and save the file in the location of your choice. The file is saved as .HTML as default.

The test can also be saved with an extension htm, shtml, and xhtml.

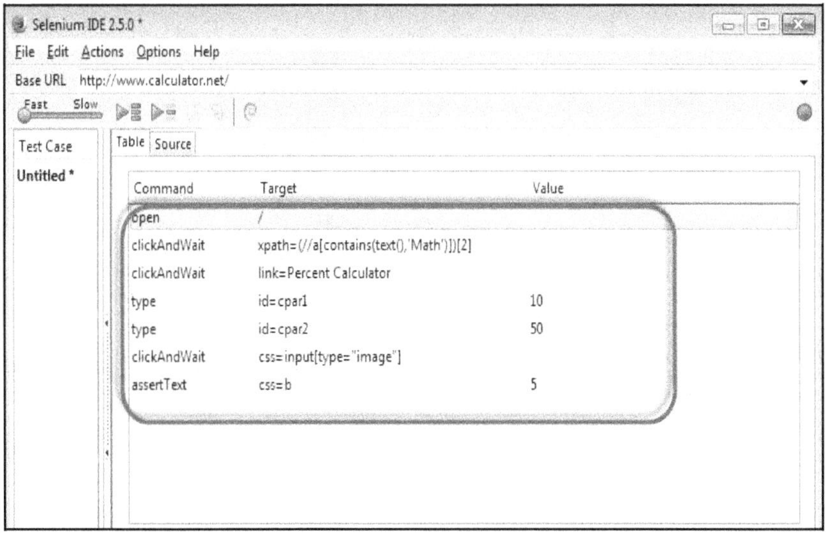

5.1.3. Saving the Test Suite

A test suite is a collection of tests that can be executed as a single entity.

Step 1 : Create a test suite by navigating to "File" >> "New Test Suite" as shown below.

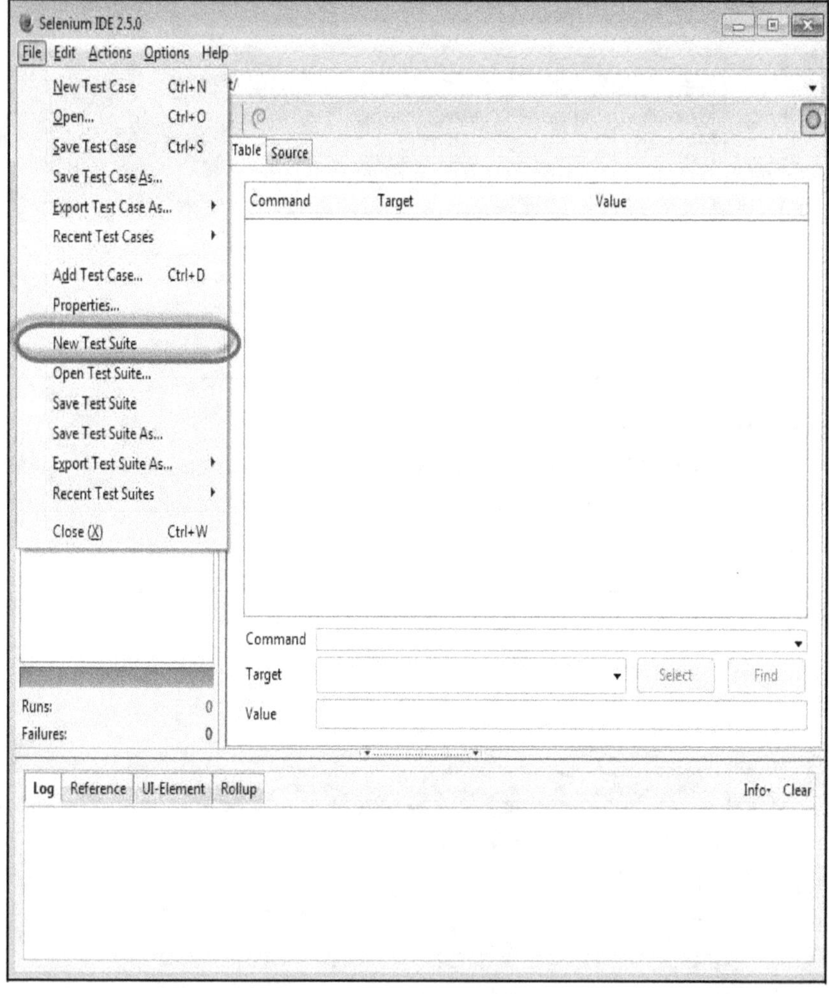

Step 2 : The tests can be recorded one by one by choosing the option "New Test Case" from the "File" Menu.

Step 3 : The individual tests are saved with a name along with saving a "Test Suite".

5.1.4. Executing the Recorded Test

The recorded scripts can then be executed either by clicking "Play entire suite" or "Play current test" button in the toolbar.

Step 1 : The Run status can be seen in the status pane that displays the number of tests passed and failed.

Step 2 : Once a step is executed, the user can see the result in the "Log" Pane.

Step 3 : After executing each step, the background of the test step turns "Green" if passed and "Red" if failed as shown below.

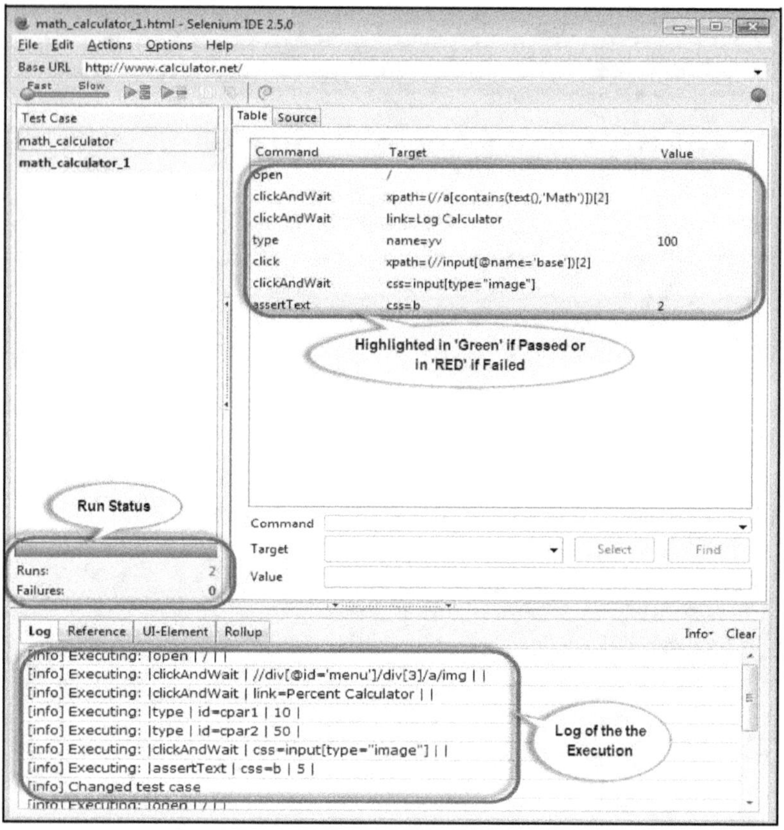

5.2. Creating Selenium Script Using Firebug

Step 1 : Launch Selenium IDE

Launch Firefox browser and then ***Selenium IDE***.

Type the base URL (***http://store.demoqa.com./***) inside the Base URL textbox.

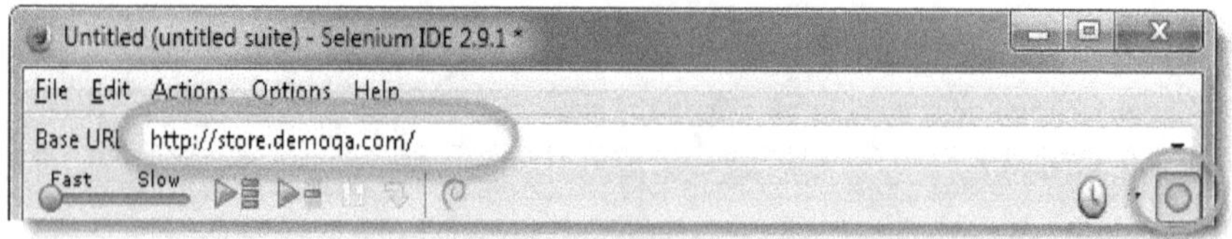

Step 2: Open URL

Click on the first empty ***test step*** in the Editor.

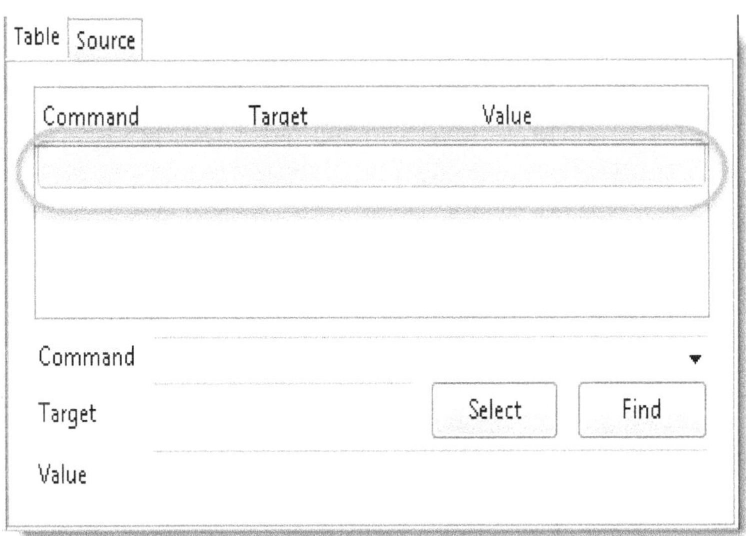

Type **open** command in the command text box. The "open" command opens the specified URL.

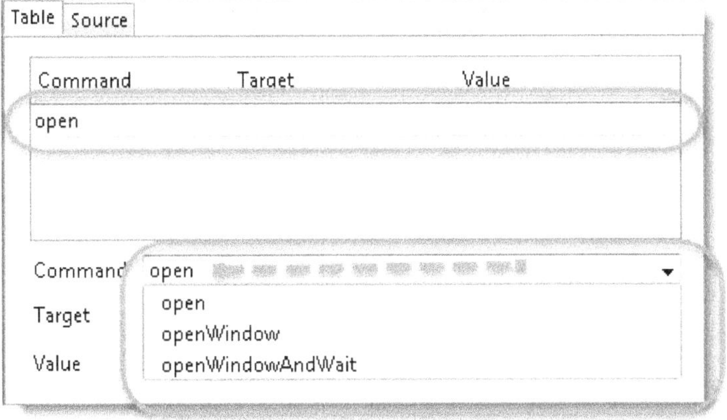

Step 3: Verify Title

Open up the **http://store.demoqa.com/** URL in the Firefox browser. Click on Firebug,

In Firebug, expand the <head> tag to display the <title> tag. Click on the value of the <title> tag.

Copy the title of the webpage which is **ONLINE STORE | Toolsqa Dummy Test site**.

Click on the second empty test step in the Editor and Type **verifyTitle** command in the command text box. *verifyTitle* command returns the current page title and compares it with the specified title.

And Paste the title copied in step 4 into the Target field of the second step.

Command	Target	Value
open		
verifyTitle	ONLINE STORE | Tools...	

Command: verifyTitle

Target: | Toolsqa Dummy Test site   Select   Find

Value:

Step 4: Click on My Account

For third command Click on the third empty test step in the Editor and Type ***clickAndWait*** command in the command text box. We shall use the *clickAndWait* command for the user to click on ***My Account*** button.

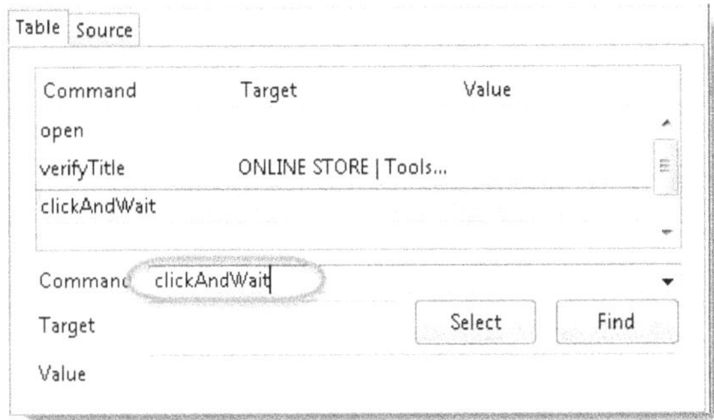

In Firebug, click on the ***Inspect*** button and then Click on the *My Account* button. Notice that Firebug automatically shows you the HTML code for that element. *My Account* button does not have any *ID or Name*. We shall, therefore, use its xpath or css as the locator.

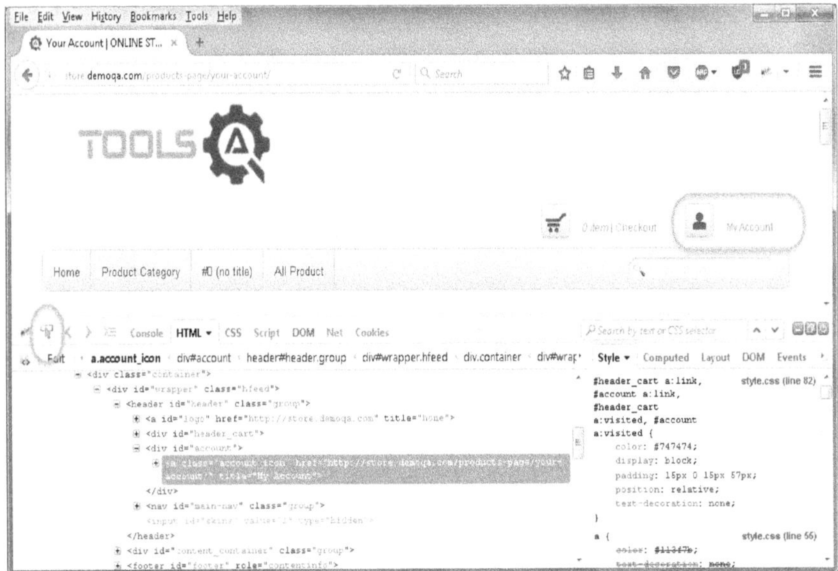

Now, Right-click the highlighted code in the Firebug panel and ***Copy the xpath*** and paste it onto the Target field in Selenium IDE.

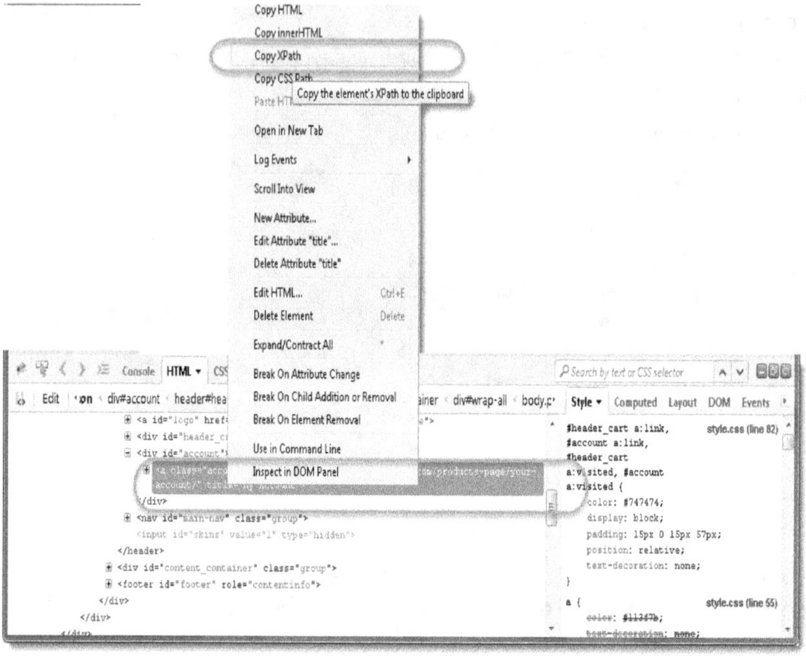

Target text box, prefix with **xpath=**, indicating that Selenium IDE should target an element whose Xpath attribute is */html/body/div[2]/div/div/header/div[2]/a*.

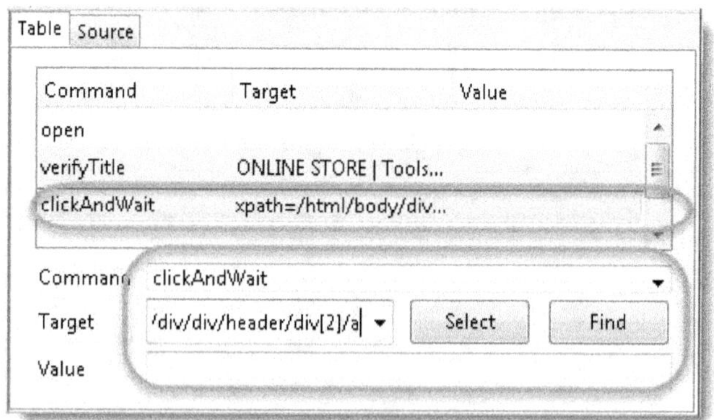

Step 5: Enter Username and Password

For fourth command Click on the fourth empty test step in the Editor and Type **type** command in the command text box.

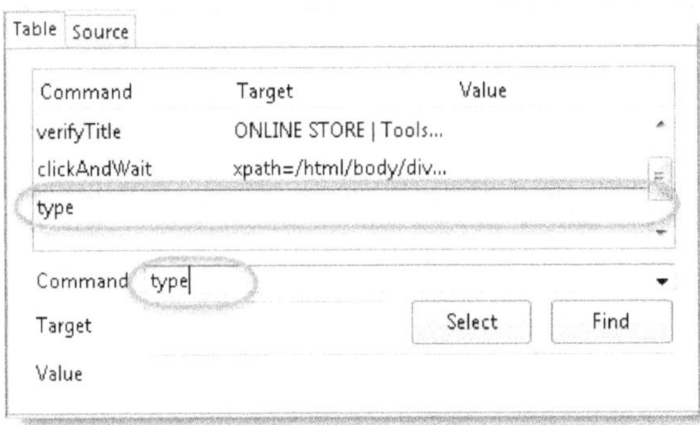

In Firebug, click on the ***Inspect*** button. Click on the ***Username*** text box. Firebug shows you the HTML code for that element.

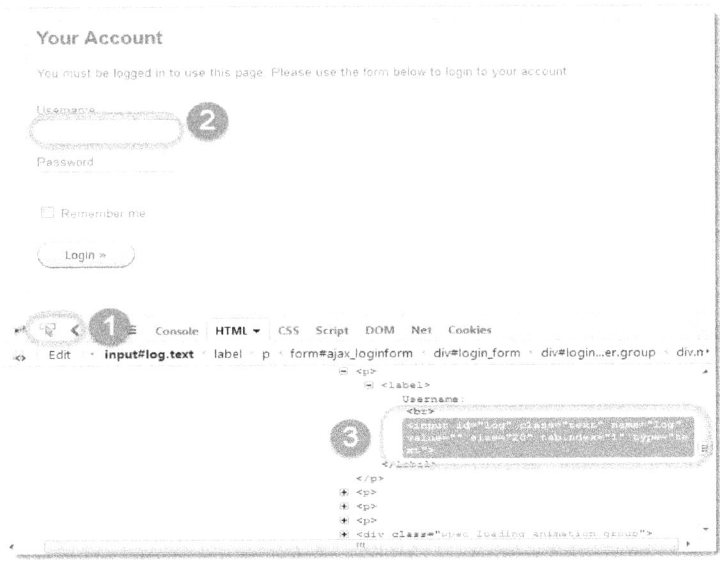

Username text box have an ID attribute. Use its ID as the locator. Copy the ID value and paste it into the Target field in Selenium IDE.

Exactly the same way make one step script for password as well.

Step 6: Click on Login

Now, we will have to click the login button. Click on the sixth empty test step in the Editor and Type ***clickAndWait*** command in the command text box. As usual we shall utilize firebug to find out an appropriate locator.

Copy the ID value and paste it into the Target field in Selenium IDE. Type your Password in the Value text box of Selenium IDE.

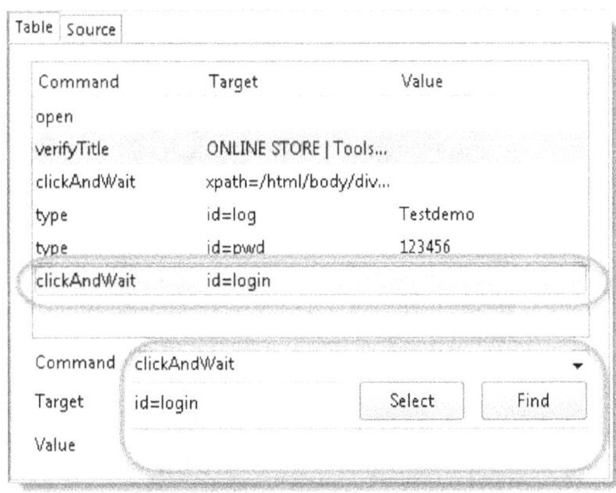

Step 7: Play Back the Script

Our test script is complete now. Save the test case and the completed script will look like As Shown in Image bellow

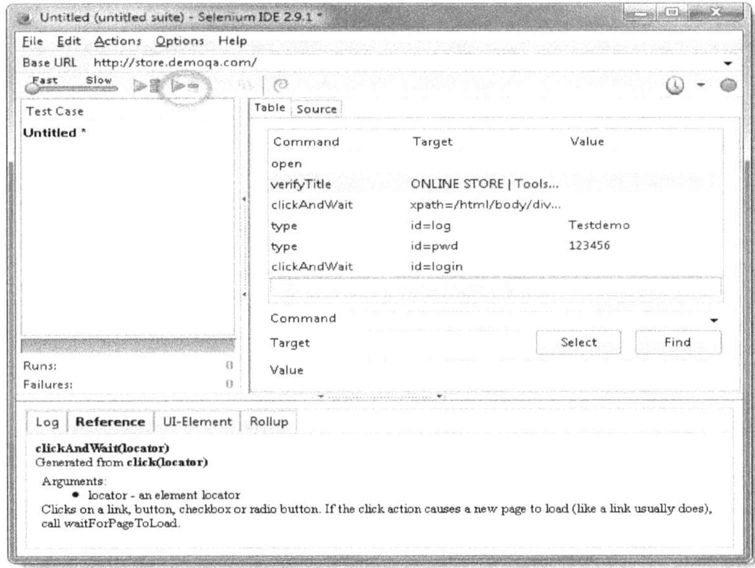

5.3.   Login Shopping Website Using Selenium IDE

1. Select Selenium Tool from mozilla firefox
2. Open the **selenium IDE**

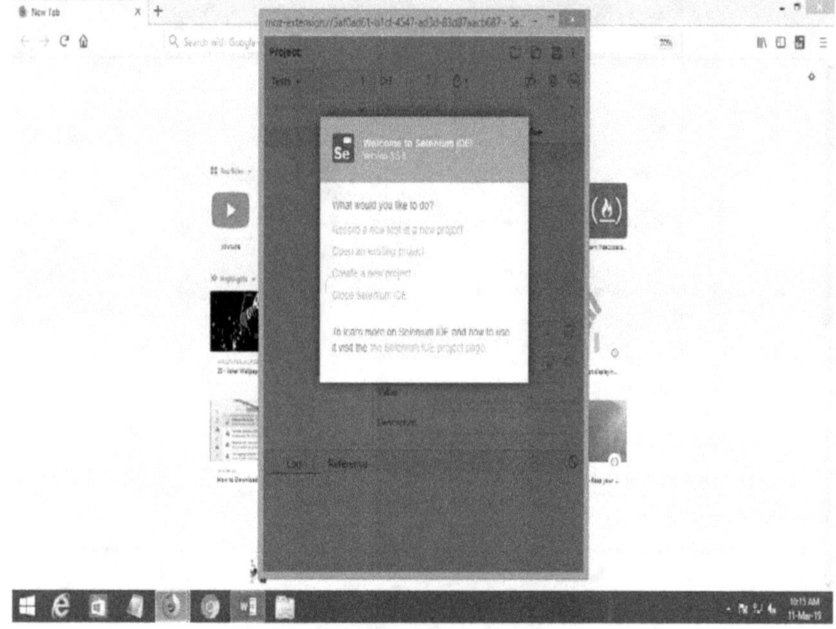

3. Click **record a new test in a new project**.

4. Enter the **project name**

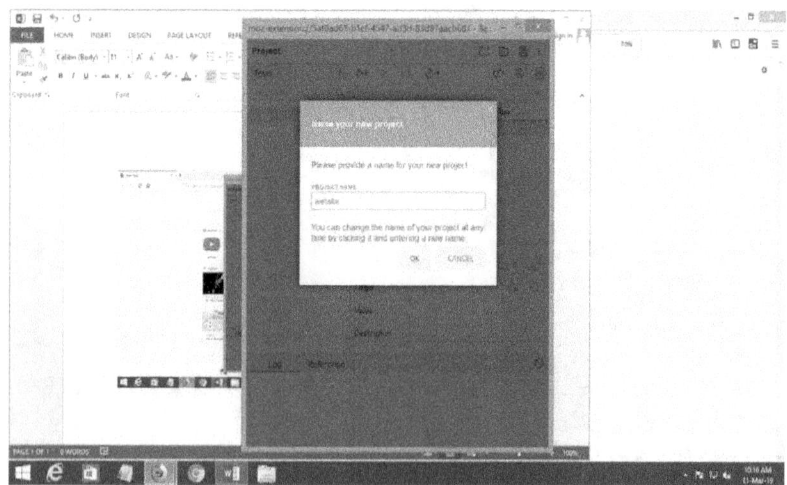

click ok.

5. Enter the URL name " **https://www.clubfactory.com**"

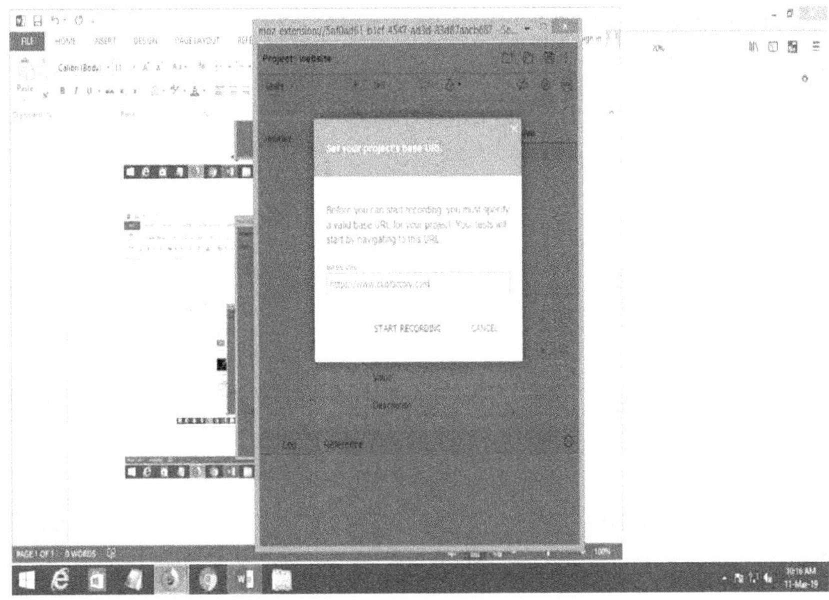

6. Click **Start Recording**.

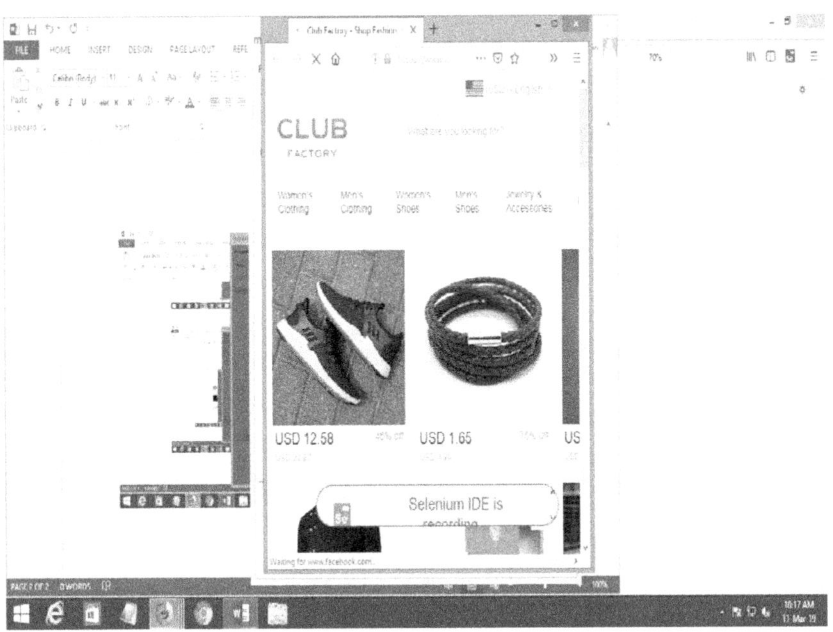

7. Close the URL www.clubfactory.com and save the test case

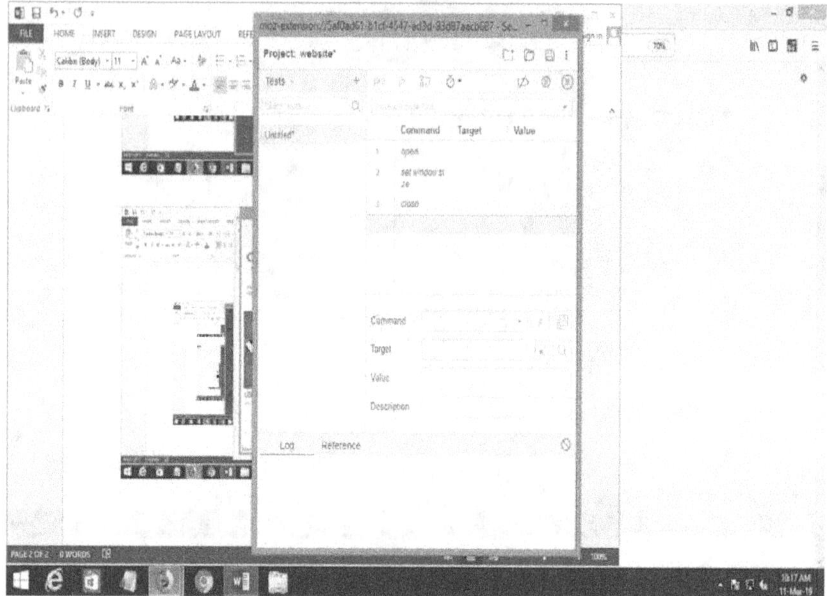

5.4.   Create a Test Case Script for Searching the Topic Using Selenium

1.   Open URL as ***https://www.google.co.in***

2.   Click *FIREBUG* and click *INSPECT ELEMENT*

3.   Click *INSPECT* and right click *TEXTBOX*

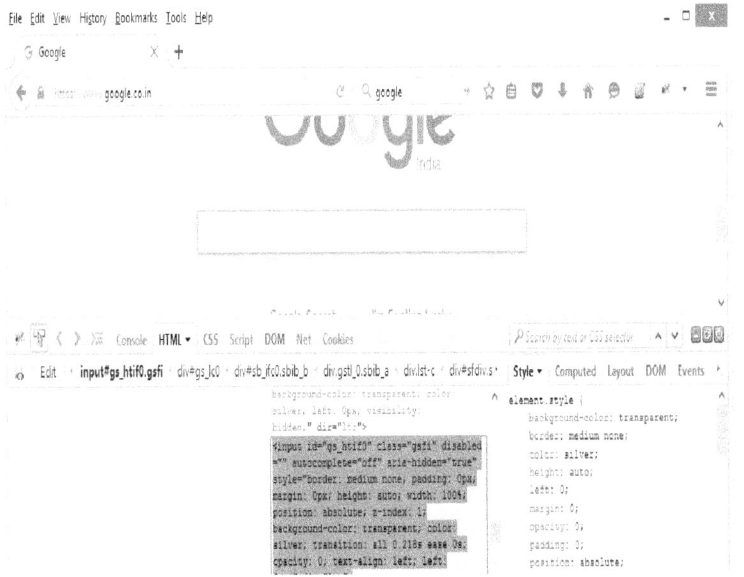

4.   Select and copy *IDproperty* of **TEXTBOX**

5.   Click ***INSPECT ELEMENT*** and right click ***Google Search BUTTON***

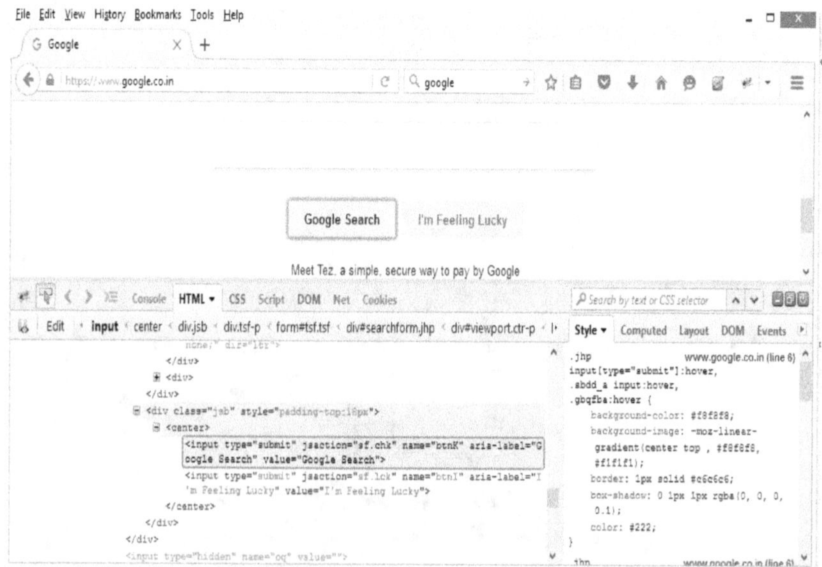

6. Select and copy *NAME* property of *Google Search BUTTON*

Selenium Test Case Script Command

COMMAND	TARGET	VALUE
open	/	https://www.google.co.in/
type	id=gs_htif0	test case design techniques
ClickAndWait	name=btnK	Google Search
ClickAndWait	link=Test Case Design Technique - TutorialsPoint	
ClickAndWait	link=Acceptance Testing	

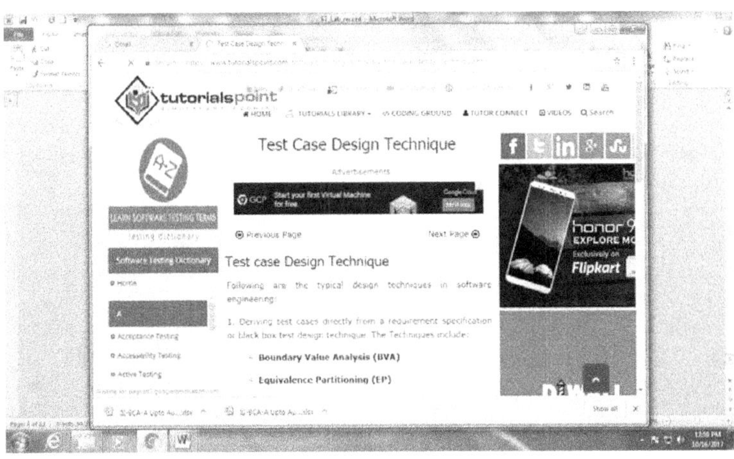

CHAPTER 6

Installing Eclipse Juno

6.1.   Download Eclipse JUNO

Step 1 : Navigate to the URL: http://www.eclipse.org/downloads/ and download the appropriate file based on your OS architecture.

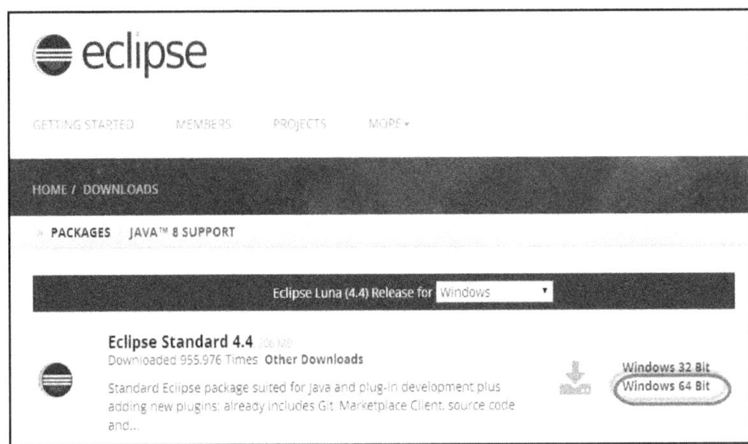

Step 2 : Click the 'Download' button.

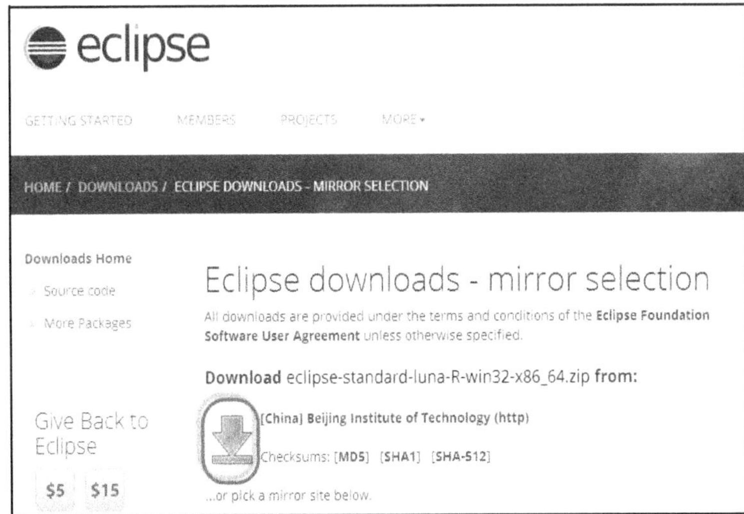

Step 3 : The download would be in a Zipped format. Unzip the contents.

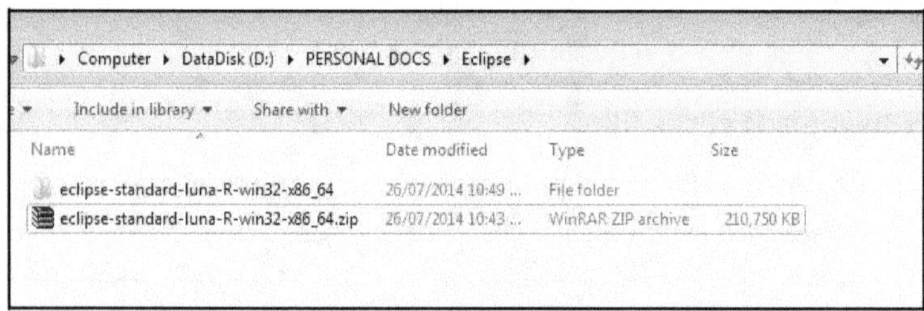

Step 4 : Locate Eclipse.exe and double click on the file.

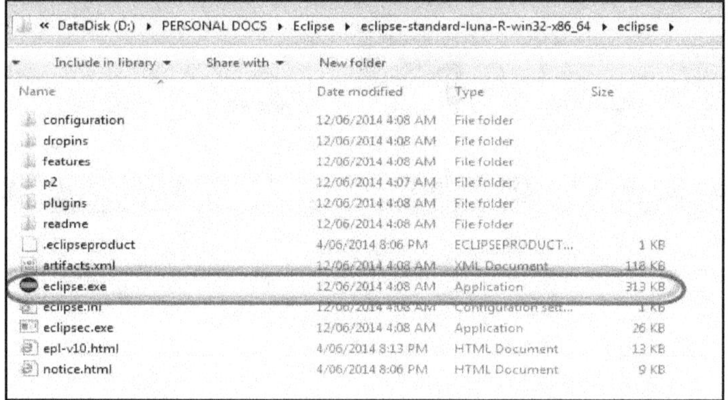

6.2.   Configure Eclipse JUNO

Step 5 : To configure the workspace, select the location where the development has to take place.

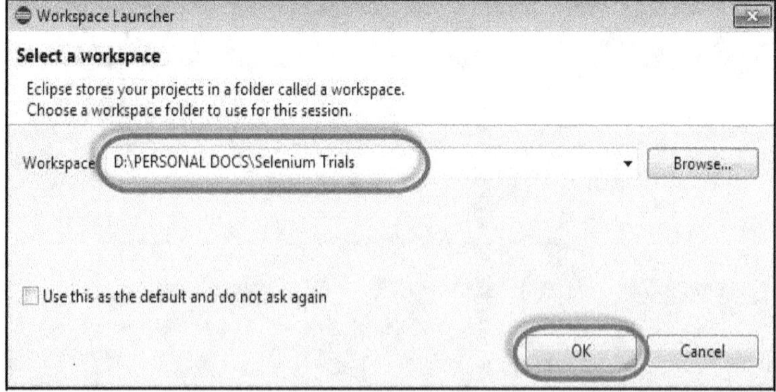

Step 6 : The Eclipse window opens as shown below.

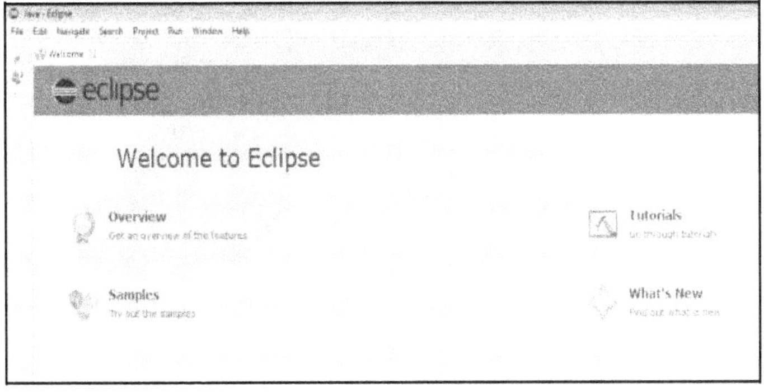

CHAPTER 7

Selenium Webdriver

7.1. Birth of WebDriver

- Simon Stewart created WebDriver circa 2006 when browsers and web applications were becoming more powerful and more restrictive with JavaScript programs like Selenium Core.

- It was the first cross-platform testing framework that could control the browser from the OS level.

7.2. Brief Introduction WebDriver

- The WebDriver proves itself to be better than both Selenium IDE and Selenium RC in many aspects.

- It implements a more modern and stable approach in automating the browser's actions.

- WebDriver, unlike Selenium RC, does not rely on JavaScript for Automation.

- It controls the browser by directly communicating with it.

The supported languages are.

- Java
- C#
- PHP
- Python
- Perl
- Ruby

7.3. Pros and Cons of Selenium WebDriver

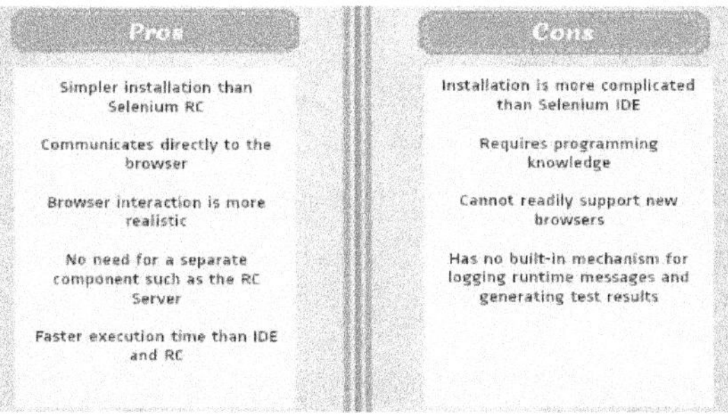

7.4. Install Web Driver - Chrome Driver

Steps to Install Selenium Web Driver – Chrome Driver

1. Open Mozilla FireFox browser and type Seleniumhq.

2. Click Selenium - Web Browser Automation.

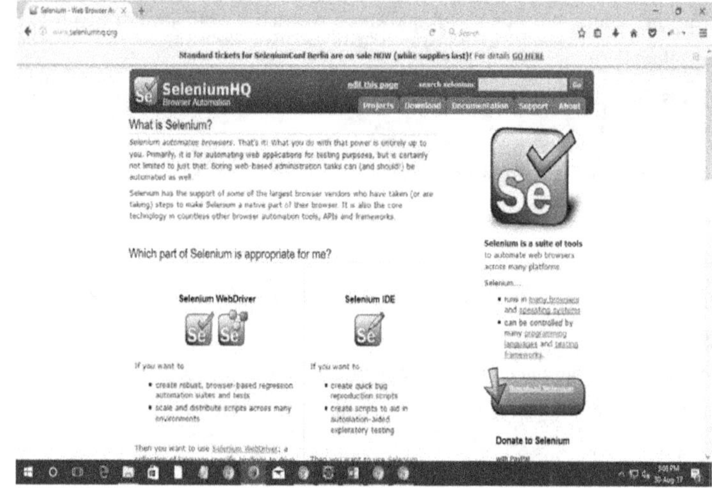

3. Click to **Download Selenium**

4. **Go to** Third Party Drivers, Bindings, and Plugins **click 2.3.1**

Google Chrome Driver

2.31

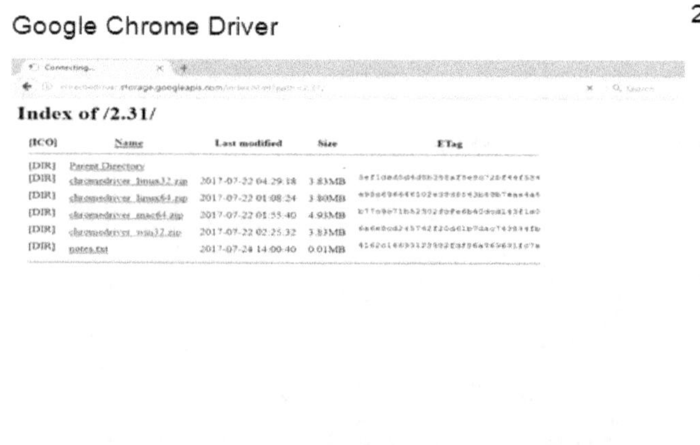

5. Click chromedriver_win32.zip

6. Store and exact the file in E: or D:

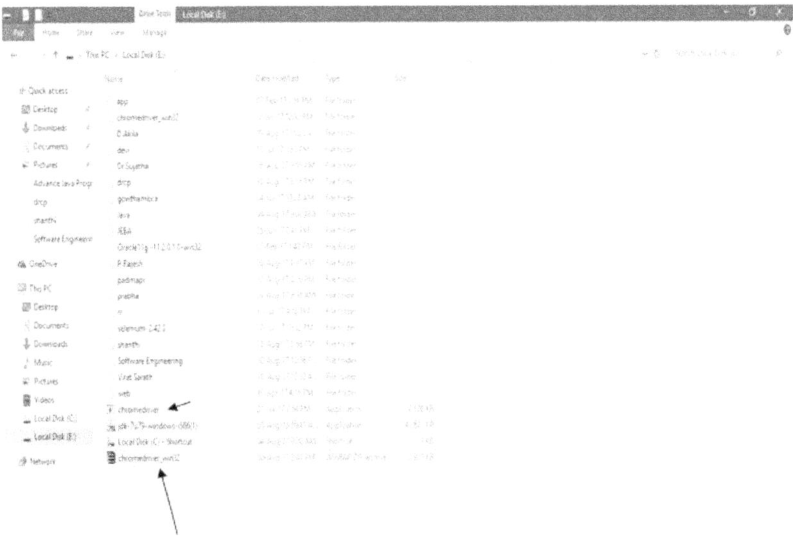

7.5.   Configure FirePath

To work with Selenium RC or WebDriver, we need to locate elements based on their XPath or ID or name, etc. In order to locate an element, we need tools/plugins.

1. FirePath, a plugin that works within Firebug, helps users to grab the 'XPath' of an element.

2. Install FirePath by navigating to "https://addons.mozilla.org/en-US/firefox/addon /firepath/"

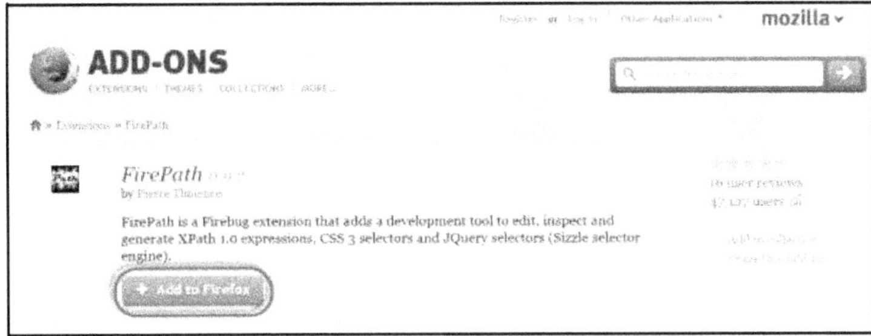

3. The add-on installer is shown to the user and it is installed upon clicking the 'Install' button.

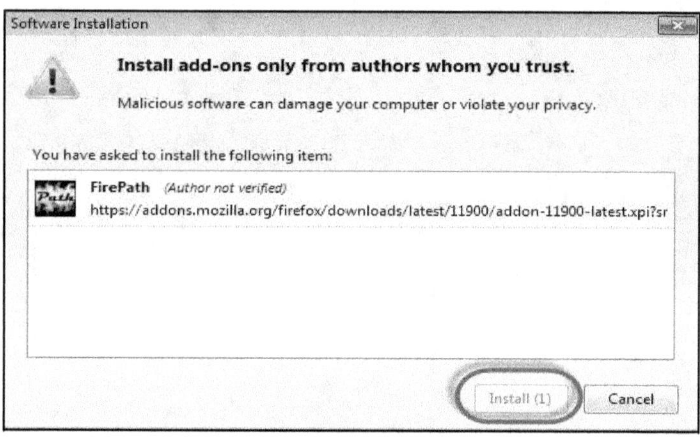

Example

Now let us understand how to use FireBug and FirePath with an example. For demonstration, we will use www.google.com and capture the properties of the text box of "google.com".

Step 1 : First click on the arrow icon as highlighted in the following screenshot and drag it to the object for which we would like to capture the properties. The HTML/DOM of the object would be displayed as shown below. We are able to capture the 'ID' of the input text box with which we can interact.

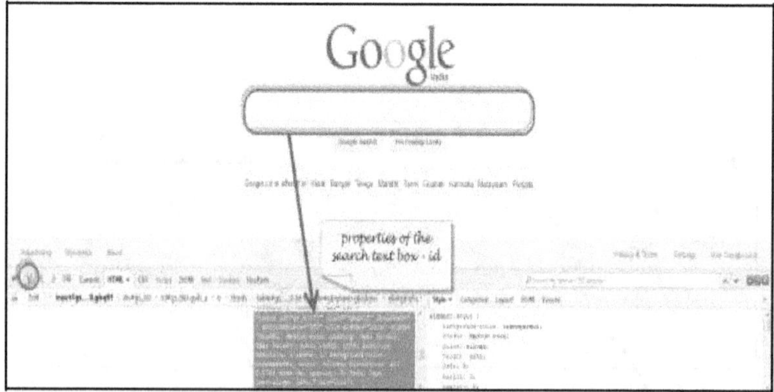

Step 2 : To fetch the XPath of the object, go to 'firepath' tab and perform the following steps.

- Click the Spy icon.
- Select the Control for which we would like to capture the XPath.
- XPath of the selected control would be generated.

CHAPTER 8

Test Automation Using Selenium Webdriver Script with Eclipse Juno

8.1. Steps to Build the Path Selenium WebDriver in Eclipse JUNO

1. Open Eclipse Icons

S

and click run button

2. Select workspace in E: or D: drive in your name (makenewfolder)

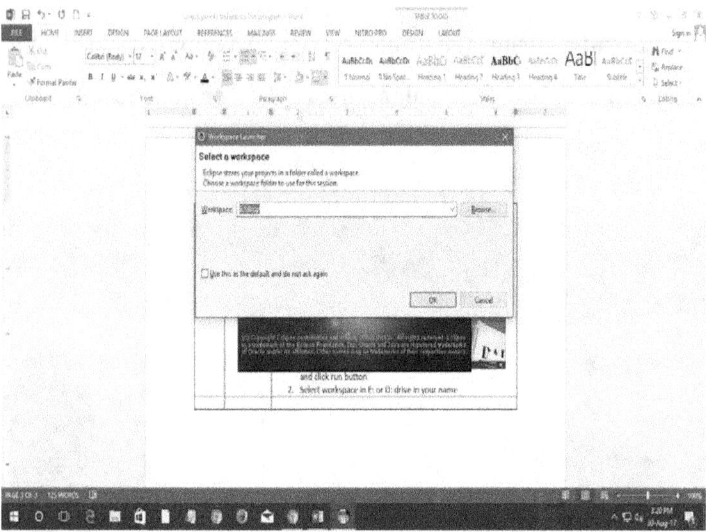

and click ok

3. Go to FILE -> NEW -> OTHER -> Java Project

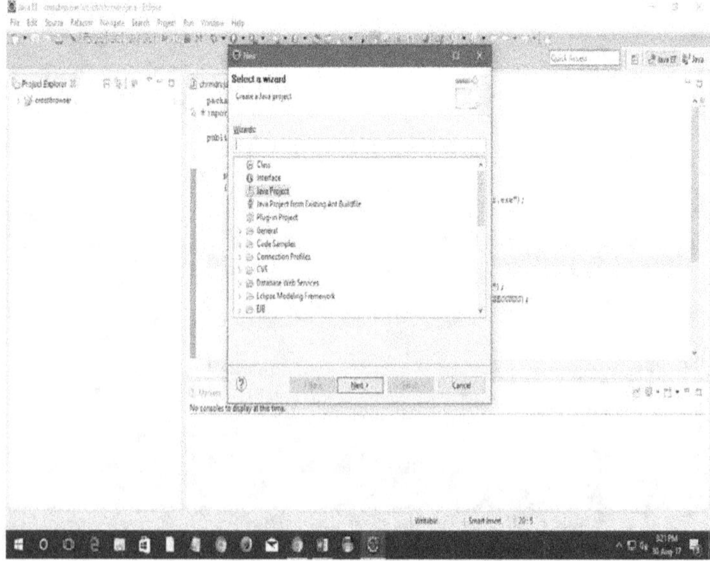

and click New.

4. Type **project name (eg. Crossbrowser)**

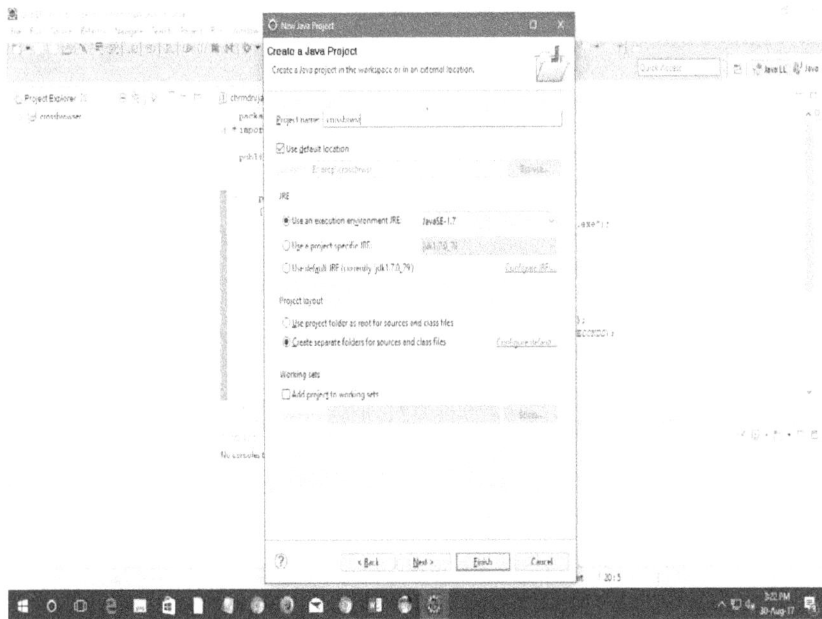

and click **Finish button**

5. Right click on **crossbrwsr -> NEW -> PACKAGE**

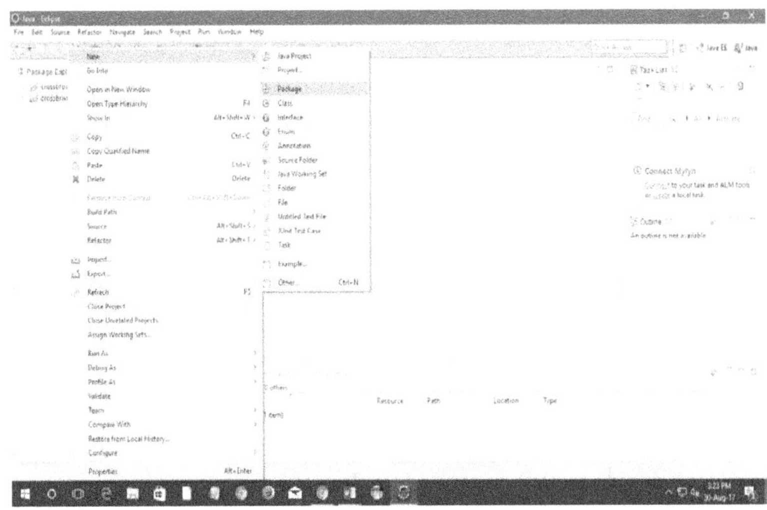

6. Type **package name as crb**

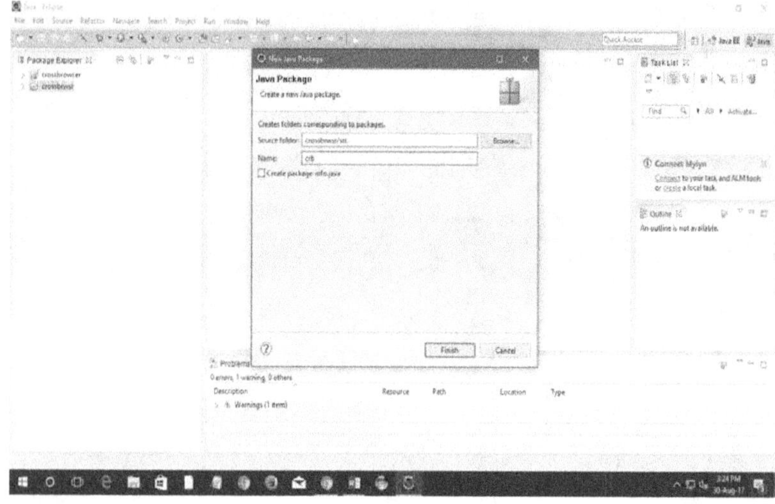

and click finish

7. Right **click on crb(package) ->NEW -> CLASS**

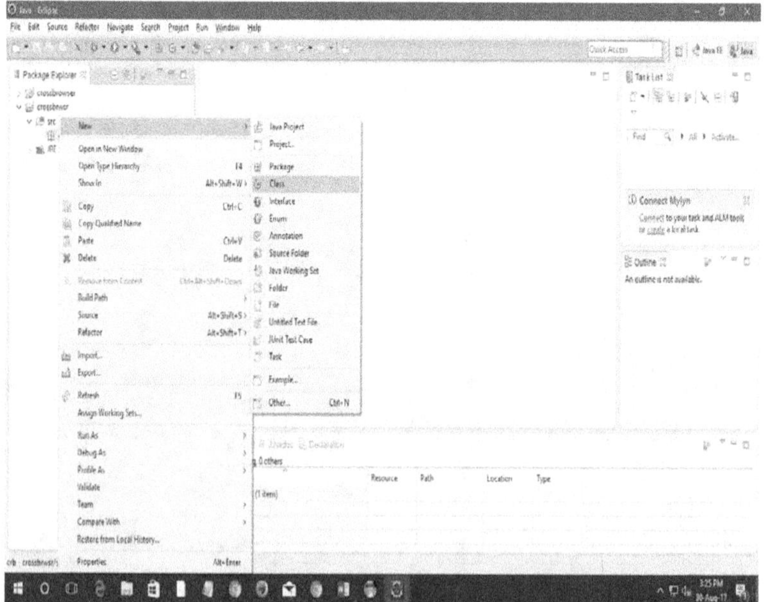

- type **class name as chromdr**
- Select **check box as Public static void main(String[] args)**

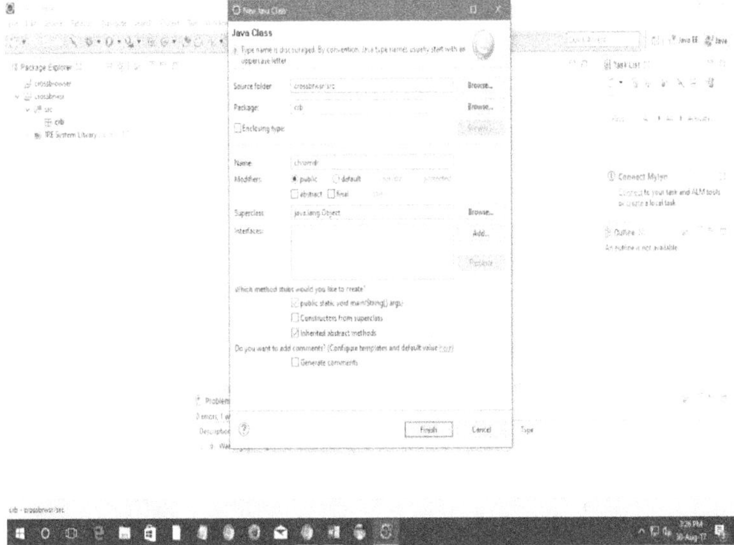

and click Finish button

8. Again **right click on crb package -> Build path -> Configure build path**

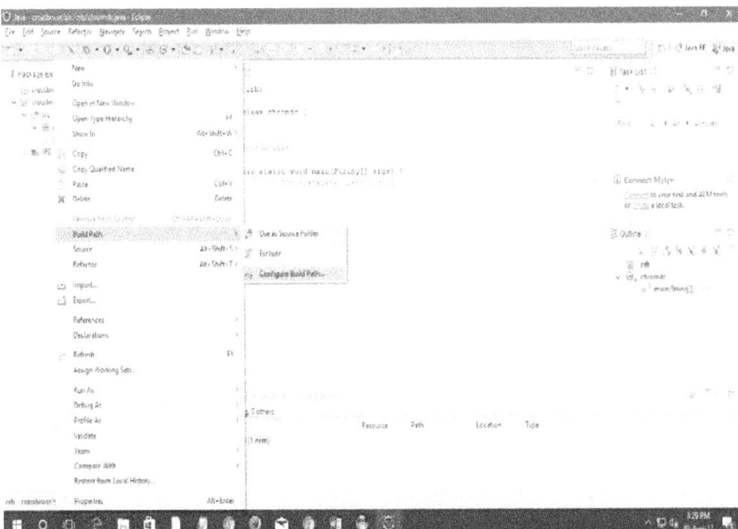

9. Select **libraries tab** and **click Add External JARs button**

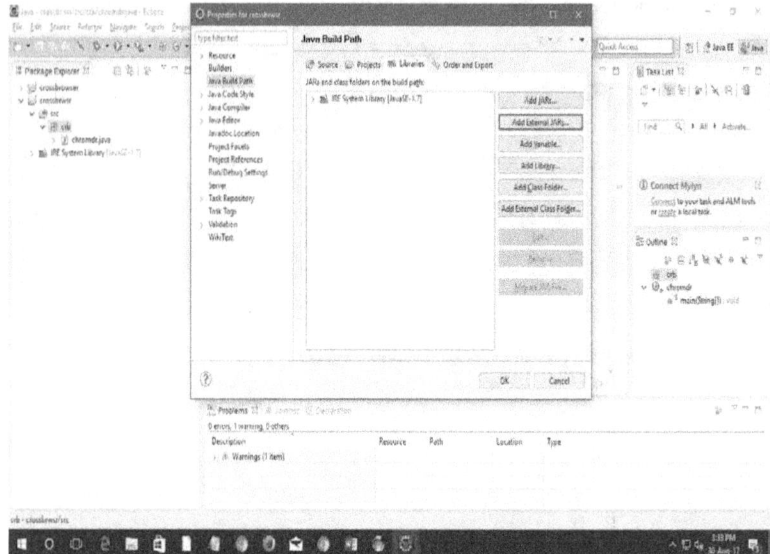

10. Select E:\selenium-2.42.0 \ selenium-java-2.42.0

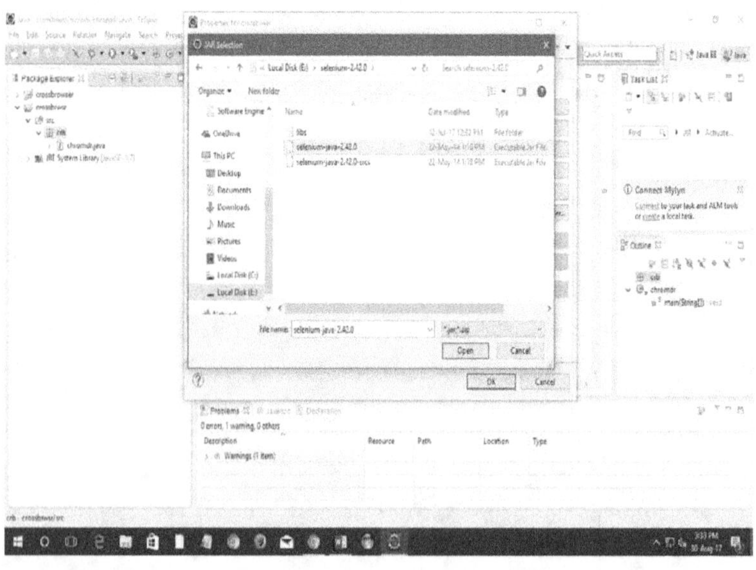

and click Open

11. Once again click Add External JARs button

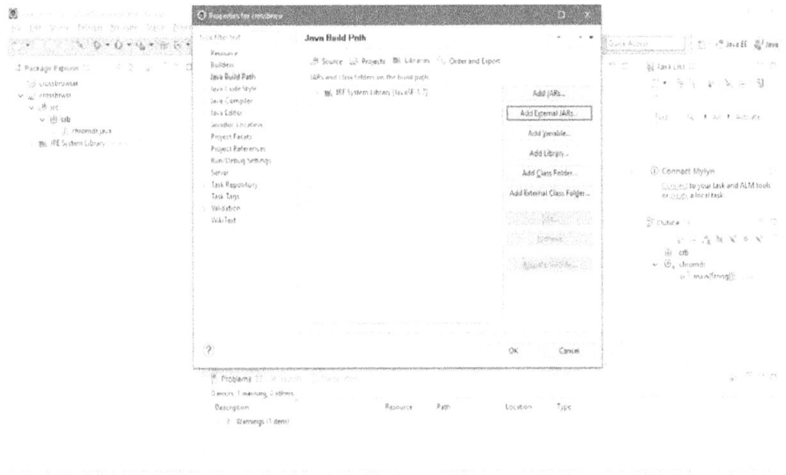

12. Select E:\selenium-2.42.0\libs and select all files from libs

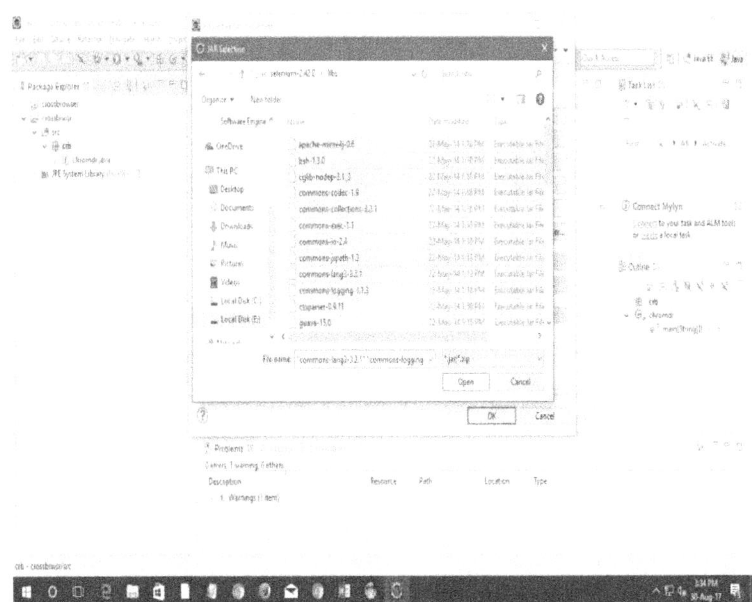

then click open and then click ok

13. Now **the** coding **screen looks in program structure**

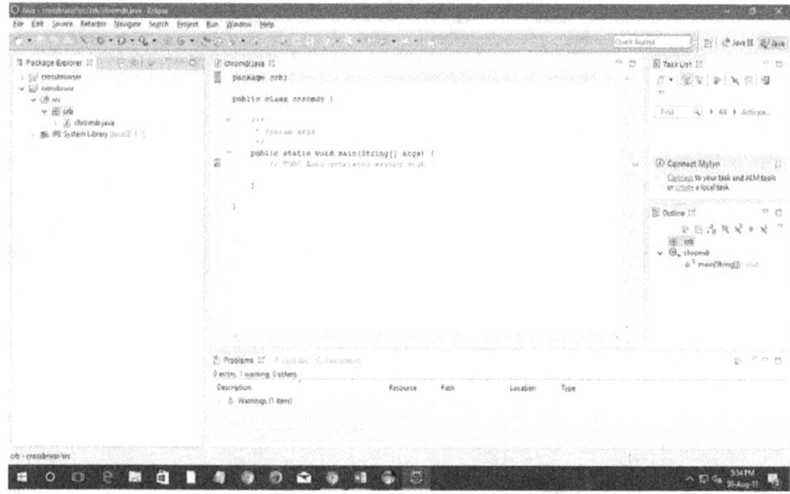

8.2.　　Cross Browser

Test a program to login a specific web page

Steps

1.　Create package and class name and add external jars of SELENIUM and its library.
2.　Create an object as driver of webdriver.
3.　Set the base url as google.com.

Coding

```
package crossbrowser;
import org.openqa.selenium.WebDriver;
import org.openqa.selenium.chrome.ChromeDriver;
import org.openqa.selenium.firefox.FirefoxDriver;
public class chrmdrv
{
  public static void main(String[] args)
  {
    System.setProperty("webdriver.chrome.driver","E:\\chromedriver.exe");
        WebDriver driver = new ChromeDriver();
        driver.get("https://google.com");
```

                        String PageTitle = driver.getTitle();
                                if(PageTitle.equals("Google"))
                {

                        System.out.println("google launch - passed");
                }

                                else
                {

                        System.out.println("google launch - fails");
                }

driver.close();
                }

}

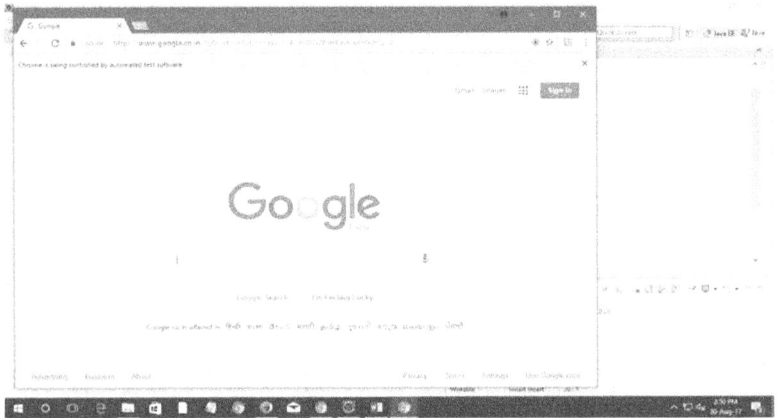

8.3.   To Compare Google's Expected Title vs. Actual Title

Steps

1.   Create package and class name and add external jars of SELENIUM and its library.
2.   Create an object as driver of web driver.
3.   Set the base Url as http:\\www.google.com.
4.   Declare the variable as String named Actual title & Expected Title.
5.   Get the Expected title from the base url by using driver. Get title method
6.   Check whether the actual title vs Expected title.

Coding

```java
package expact;
import org.openqa.selenium.WebDriver;
import org.openqa.selenium.chrome.ChromeDriver;
import org.openqa.selenium.firefox.FirefoxDriver;
public class etat
{
  public static void main(String[] args)
  {
        System.setProperty("webdriver.chrome.driver","E:\\chromedriver.exe");
            WebDriver driver = new ChromeDriver();

        String appUrl ="https://google.com";
        driver.get(appUrl);
        driver.manage().window().maximize();
        String expectedTitle = "Google";
        String actualTitle = driver.getTitle();
        if (expectedTitle.equals(actualTitle))
        {
          System.out.println("Verification Successful - The Expected Title is displayed on the web page.");
        }
        else
        {
          System.out.println("Verification Failed - The Expected Title is not displayed on the web page.");
        }
            driver.close();
        }
}
```

8.4.   Login Gmail Account with Username and Password

Steps

1. Create package and class name and add external jars of SELENIUM and its library.
2. Create an object as driver of web driver.
3. Set the base Url as http:\\www.google.com.
4. Find an element by using its id named email and password which sends a text later.
5. Find an element by using its id named NEXT and CLICK.

Coding

```
package Login;
import java.util.concurrent.TimeUnit;
import org.openqa.selenium.By;
import org.openqa.selenium.WebDriver;
import org.openqa.selenium.chrome.ChromeDriver;
import org.openqa.selenium.firefox.FirefoxDriver;
public class Glogin
{
        public static void main(String[] args)
    {
        System.setProperty("webdriver.chrome.driver","E:\\chromedriver.exe");
WebDriver driver = new ChromeDriver();
    String appurl="https://accounts.google.com";
        driver.get(appurl);
        driver.manage().window().maximize();
    driver.findElement(By.id("Email")).sendKeys("pri.gcbabu");
    driver.manage().timeouts().implicitlyWait(60, TimeUnit.SECONDS);
    driver.findElement(By.id("next")).click();
        driver.findElement(By.id("Passwd")).sendKeys("********");
        driver.findElement(By.id("signIn")).click();
    driver.close();
    System.out.println("test script element successfully");
        System.exit(0);
    }
 }
```

Output

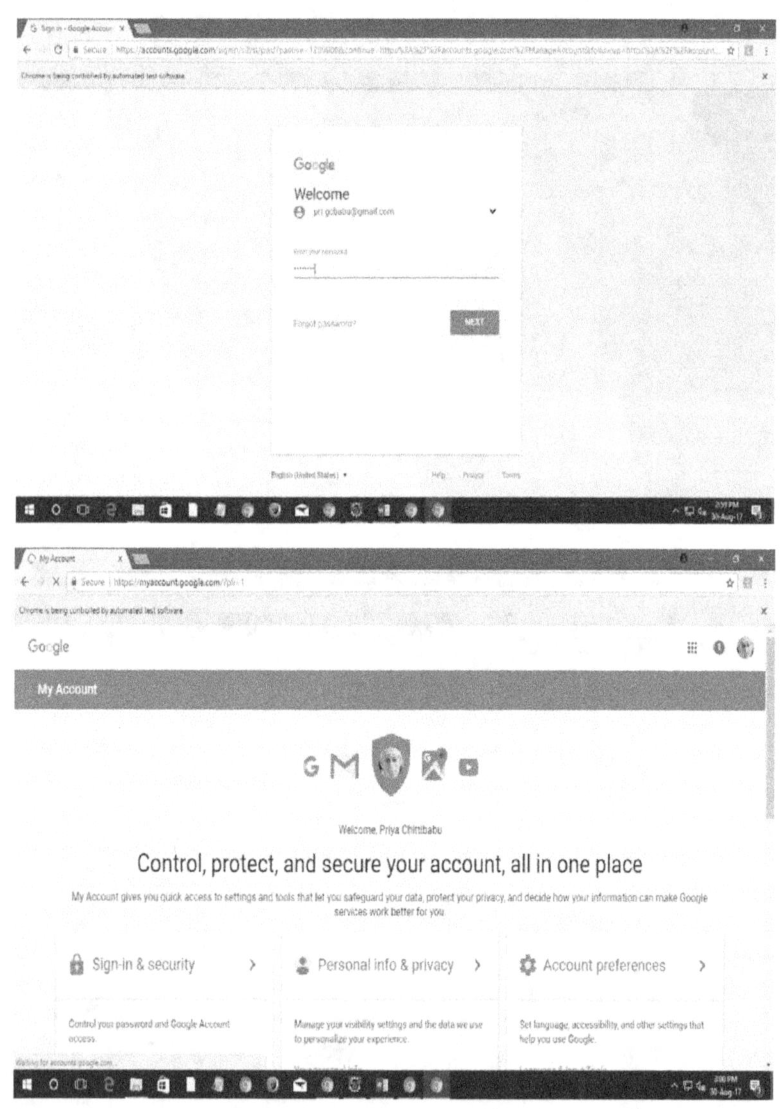

Google
Welcome
pri.gcbabu@gmail.com
Enter your password
Forgot password?
NEXT
English (United States)
Help   Privacy   Terms

Google
My Account
G M
Welcome, Priya Chintibabu
Control, protect, and secure your account, all in one place
My Account gives you quick access to settings and tools that let you safeguard your data, protect your privacy, and decide how your information can make Google services work better for you

Sign-in & security   >
Personal info & privacy   >
Account preferences   >

Control your password and Google Account access.
Manage your visibility settings and the data we use to personalize your experience.
Set language, accessibility, and other settings that help you use Google.

CHAPTER 9

TestNG

9.1. Introduction

TestNG is a testing framework inspired from JUnit and NUnit but introducing some new functionalitiesthatmake itmorepowerfulandeasiertouse,suchas:

- Annotations.
- Runyourtestsinarbitrarilybigthreadpoolswithvariouspoliciesavailable (all methods in their own thread, one thread per test class, etc...).
- Test that your code is multithread safe.
- Flexible test configuration.
- Support for data-driven testing (with @DataProvider).
- Support for parameters.
- Powerful execution model (no more TestSuite).
- Supportedbyavarietyoftoolsandplug-ins (Eclipse, IDEA, Maven, etc...).
- Embeds BeanShell for further flexibility.
- Default JDK functions for runtime and logging (no dependencies).
- Dependent methods for application server testing.

TestNG is designed to cover all categories of tests: unit, functional, end-to-end, integration, etc...

9.2. Installing TestNG in Eclipse

- Select *Help / Software updates / Find andInstall.*
- Search *for new features to install.*
- *New remote site.*
- For Eclipse 3.4 and above, enter http://beust.com/eclipse.
- For Eclipse 3.3 and below, enter http://beust.com/eclipse1.
- Make sure the check box next to URL is checked and click *Next.*
- Eclipse will then guide you through the process.

Launching your Tests in Eclipse

- We finished writing our tests, now how can we run them?

- You can launch TestNG from the command line, using a Eclipse plugin or even programatically. We are going to use the Eclipse plugin. Follow the steps described on the official TestNG documentation over here

- If you installed TestNG correctly, you will see this menu when you right click on the XML file:

- Click on "Run as TestNG Suite" and your test will start running. You will then see this nice resultstree:

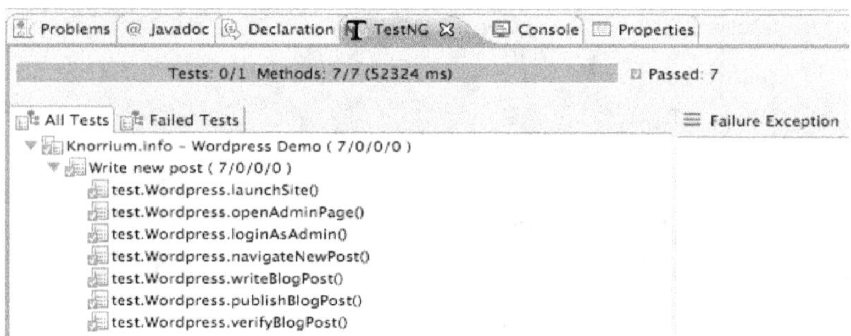

9.3. To Perform a Simple Task Using Iframe

1. Create package and class name and add external jars of SELENIUM and its library.

2. Create an object as driver of web driver.

3. Set the base url as (http://www.w3schools.com/js/tryit.asp?filename=tryjs_prompt)

4. Switch to frame driver.

5. Alert driver to switch using sendkeys.

6. Find an element Demo to get the text that contains B.sc IT.

Coding

```
package frame;
import org.openqa.selenium.Alert;
import org.openqa.selenium.By;
import org.openqa.selenium.WebDriver;
import org.openqa.selenium.chrome.ChromeDriver;
public class frame
```

```java
{
    public static void main(String[] args)
    {
        System.setProperty("webdriver.chrome.driver","D:\\chromedriver.exe");
    WebDriver driver=new ChromeDriver();


 driver.get("http://www.w3schools.com/js/tryit.asp?filename=tryjs_prompt");
 driver.manage().window().maximize();


 driver.switchTo().frame(driver.findElement(By.id("iframeResult")));
 driver.findElement(By.cssSelector("body > button")).click();
  Alert al= driver.switchTo().alert();
        al.sendKeys("B.sc[IT]");
        al.accept();


System.out.println(driver.findElement(By.id("demo")).getText().contains("B.sc[IT]"));


        driver.close();


    }
}
```

Output

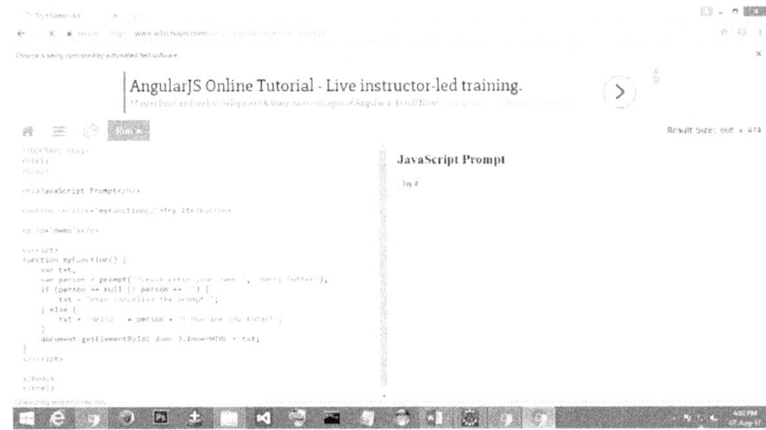

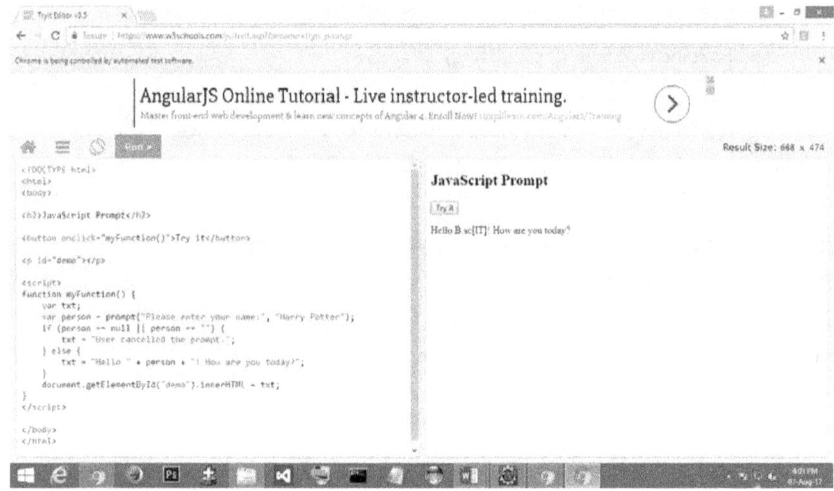

9.4. Selenium Tests with Microsoft Excel

- Parameterizing a test from external sources such as Microsoft Excel is always recommended in order to handle large amount of test data.

- To read data from Excel, we need APIs which support opening file, reading data, and writing data into Excel.

- Various classes and methods which support above mentioned operations. In this post, let us try to figure out which is the API that supports all the activities we need to do during execution of a test.

Jxl.jar is an open source Java API which supports read Excel spreadsheets and to write into Excel spreadsheets. Below are some of the operations that we can handle with this API.

1. Read data from Excel spreadsheet
2. Read and write formulas into spreadsheets
3. Generate spreadsheets
4. Supports formatting of font, number, and date
5. Supports coloring of cells

To access the methods and classes provided by this API inside Eclipse we need to add this JAR file to the Java Build Path. (I have explained steps to add external Jar files to Java Build Path in previous posts)

Download the jxl.jar from "http://jexcelapi.sourceforge.net/" Add the JAR file to Java Build Path.

Add import statements to the .java file as below to read from an Excel spreadsheet import jxl.Cell;

import jxl.Sheet; import jxl.Workbook;

import jxl.read.biff.BiffException;

9.5.   Example

Write and **test a program to select the number of students who have scored more than 60 in any one subject (or all subjects).**

import java.io.FileInputStream;

import java.io.FileOutputStream;

import jxl.Sheet;

import jxl.Workbook;

 import jxl.write.Label;

import jxl.write.WritableSheet;

import jxl.write.WritableWorkbook;

import org.testng.annotations.*;

public class exp7

{

@BeforeClass

public void setUp() **throws** Exception {

}

@Test

public void testImportexport1() **throws** Exception

{

 FileInputStream   fi   =   **new**   FileInputStream("D:\\exp6.xls");   Workbook   w   =
Workbook.*getWorkbook*(fi);

Sheet s = w.getSheet(0);

String a[][] = **new** String[s.getRows()][s.getColumns()];

FileOutputStream fo = **new** FileOutputStream("D://exp7Result.xls"); WritableWorkbook wwb =
Workbook.*createWorkbook*(fo);

```java
WritableSheet ws = wwb.createSheet("result", 0);
int c=0;
for(int i=0;i<s.getRows();i++)
{
 for(int j=0;j<s.getColumns();j++)
 {


if(i >= 1)
{
String b= new String();

b=s.getCell(3,i).getContents();
int x= Integer.parseInt(b);

if( x < 60)
{
c ++;
break;
}
}


a[i][j] = s.getCell(j, i).getContents();
Label l2 = new Label(j, i-c, a[i][j]); ws.addCell(l2);


}
}
wwb.write();
wwb.close();
}
}
```

Input

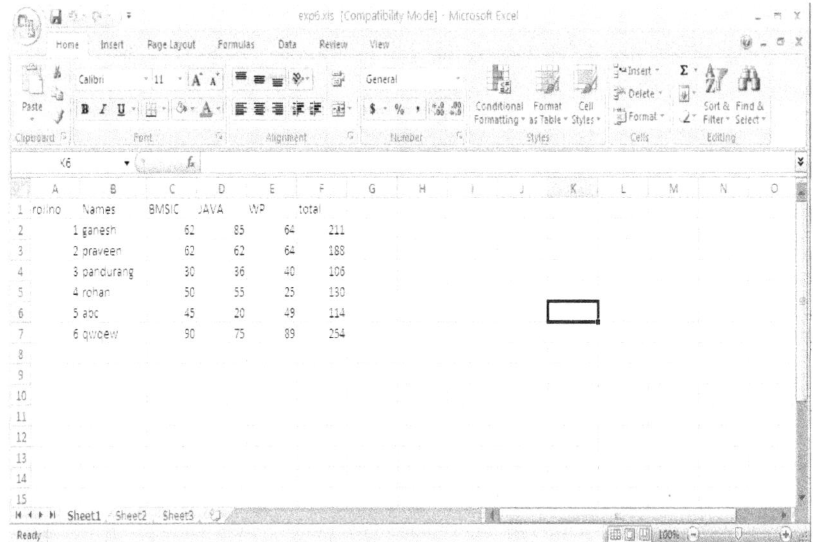

Output

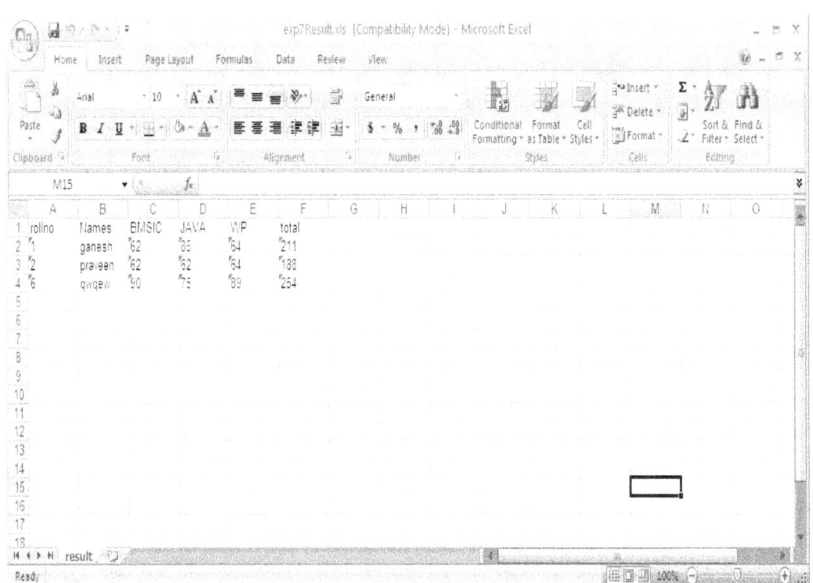

CHAPTER 10

Selenium-RC

10.1. Introduction

- Selenium-RC(Remote Control) is the solution for tests that need more than simple browser actions and linear execution
- Selenium-RC uses the full power of programming languages to create more complex tests like reading and writing files, querying a database, emailing test results
- Selenium RC was the flagship testing framework of the whole Selenium project for a long time
- Selenium RC can support the following programming languages:
  - Java
  - C#
  - PHP
  - Python
  - Perl
  - Ruby

10.2. Pros and Cons of Selenium RC

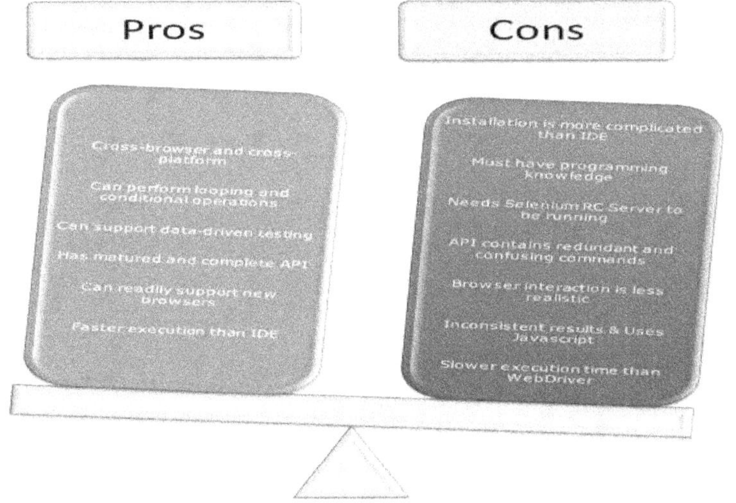

10.3. Installation of Selenium RC and Eclipse

Download Eclipse

1. Go to URL –http://www.eclipse.org/downloads/
2. Select Eclipse IDE for Java Developers (Click on Windows 32 bit platform)
3. Click on OK button and save to a local drive (i.e. C: or D:, etc)
4. Unzip the downloaded zip file and rename that to **Eclipse**
5. Create one more folder "Eclipse-Workspace" (i.e. C:Eclipse-Workspace)in the same drive where Eclipse is unzipped and renamed.
6. Create Eclipse desktop shortcut (go to C:Eclipse folder –> right click Eclipse.exe and then click on "desktop create shortcut") as demonstrated in the below pictures.

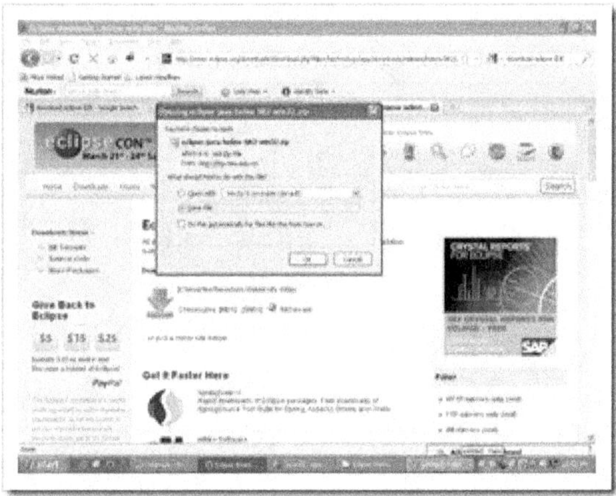

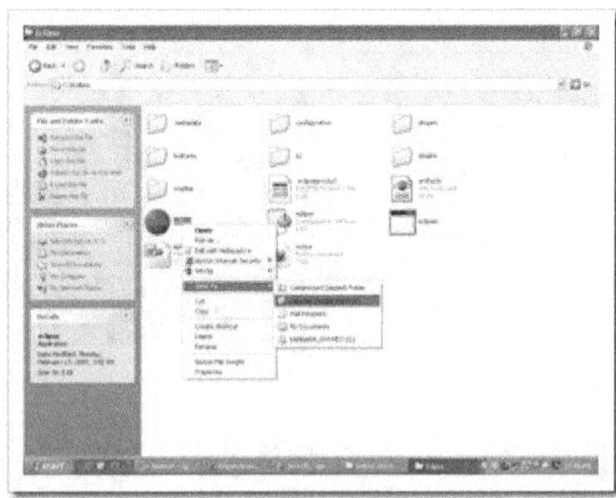

1. Now we need to create a workspace folder –> C:Eclipse- WorkspaceSeleniumTests

2. Double click on "Eclipse shortcut on Desktop"

3. This opens the Eclipse

4. Close Eclipse welcome screen

5. Click File menu –> Switch Worspace –> other

6. Now Select the C:Eclipse-WorkspaceSeleniumTests folder (These steps are demonstrated in the following figure)

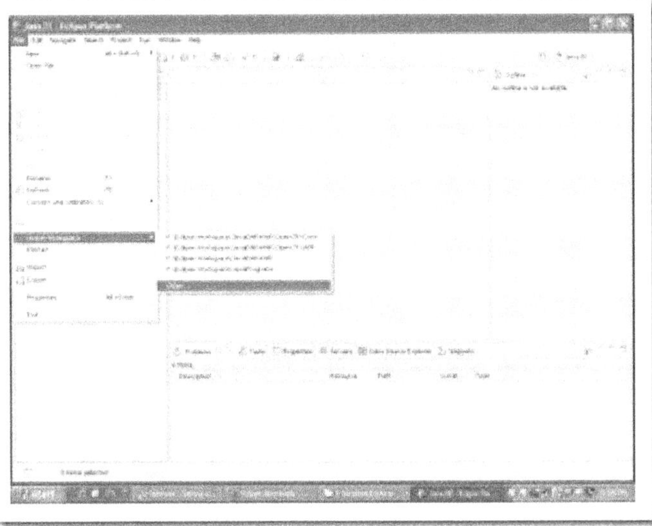

Finish to setup the eclipse.

Now, download SeleniumRC server / client driver and configure that to Eclipse

1. Download Selenium server: http://seleniumhq.org/download/

2. Download Selenium Client driver for Java (from Selenium Client Drivers section)

3. Create "Selenium" folder in C: drive and copy the Selenium-server.jar as well as unzip the Selenium Client driver (C:Selenium)

Downloading and unzipping the files into a folder is done. Configure the appropriate Selenium Client driver Jar file to the Eclipse.

1. Go to Eclipse –> Click File –> New –> Project (from various options need to select just "project")

2. In Select Wizard –> Click Java –> "Java Project" (demonstrated in the below figure).

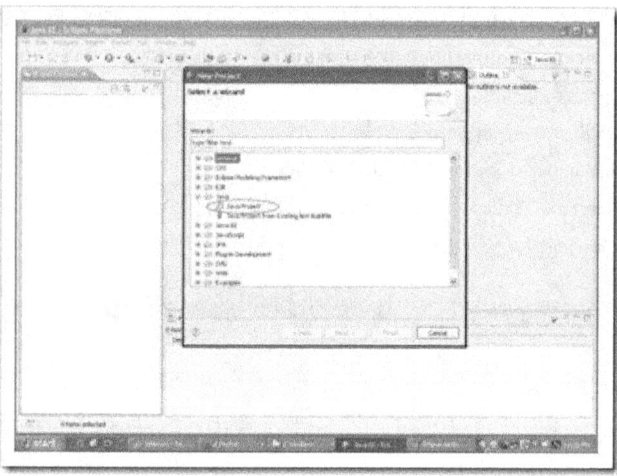

3. Give the project name (e.g. SugarCRMTests)

4. Click Finish – ClickYes

5. Done with creation of project and need to configure the Selenium Client driver to this Project

6. Right Click "SugarCRMTests" project

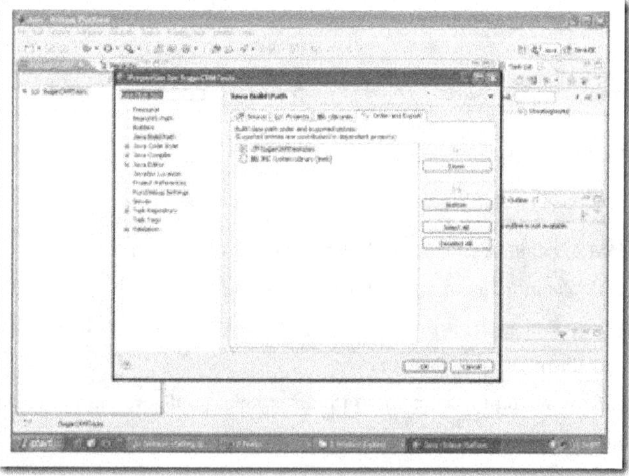

7. Click "Java Build Path"

8. Click Libraries tab

9. Click "Add External JARs" button

10. Select "Selenium Client Drivers" unzipped in C:Selenium folder (Selenium Server JAR file should not be added)

11. Click OK

12. Referenced libraries –> contains both the Selenium Client driver jar files as shown in the below picture.

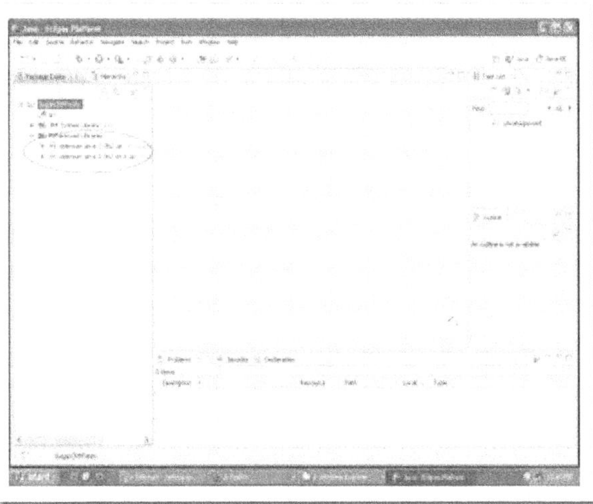

10.4. First Script-Selenium RC-JUnit-Java

Selenium RC allows to write the automated tests in any language. Selenium Scripts can be written in various ways:

1. Extending the Selenese TestCase

2. Extending the TestCase-Junit and defining an object to the DefaultSelenium Class

Before you start with your script, the following are the steps that should be performed.

Method 1: Extending the Selenese Test Case

1. Install any IDE (Eclipse, IntelliJ, IDEA), create a project.

2. Download the selenium RC file from Selenium website.

3. Extract the selenium-remote-control-1.0.3.zip file and add the selenium- remote-control-1.0.3\selenium-java-client-driver-1.0.1\selenium-java- clientdriver.jar and selenium-remote-control-1.0.3\selenium-server- 1.0.3\selenium-server.jar file to the build path.

4. Create a new package and a class in the newly created package.

5. Copy the below code:

```java
import com.thoughtworks.selenium.SeleneseTestCase;
public class SeleniumTest1 extends SeleneseTestCase
{
public void setUp() throws Exception
{
setUp("http://www.hexbytes.com/", "*firefox");
}
public void testNew() throws Exception
{
selenium.open("/"); selenium.type("searchbox", "selenium rc");
selenium.click("css=input[type='submit'][value='Search']");
selenium.waitForPageToLoad("30000"); assertTrue(selenium.isTextPresent("selenium rc"));
}
}
```

1. Start the selenium Server.
2. Click on the RunAs button and run the script as JUnit Test. If you don't find the option Install the JUnit plug-in and run the script.

Method2: Extending the Default Selenium Class

Some times we need the selenium scripts to contact the server running on a different port and different machine. You can configure the selenium scripts to handle such situations easily by extending your selenium script from TestCase(Junit) and defining the selenium instance as an object to DefaultSelenium class.

```java
package test;
import junit.framework.*;
import com.thoughtworks.selenium.DefaultSelenium; public class DefaultSelenium1 extends
TestCase{ private DefaultSelenium selenium;
public void testing()
{
selenium=new
DefaultSelenium("localhost",4444,"*iexplore","http://hexbytes.com");
selenium.start();
selenium.open("/");
selenium.type("searchbox", "selenium rc");
selenium.click("css=input[type='submit'][value='Search']");
```

selenium.waitForPageToLoad("30000");

Assert.assertTrue(selenium.isTextPresent("selenium rc"));

}

}

10.5. To handle Keyboards of a Google Chrome Driver

1. Create package and class name and add external jars of SELENIUM and its library.
2. Create an object as driver of web driver.
3. Set the base Url as http:\\www.google.com.
4. Create an web element OWE and find the element named ABOUT,create an Action object.
5. Move the element by using Action object to the selected link.
6. Send the command keys and perform the action.

```java
package handkeybrd;
import java.util.List;
import java.util.concurrent.TimeUnit;
import org.openqa.selenium.By;
import org.openqa.selenium.WebDriver;
import org.openqa.selenium.WebElement;
import org.openqa.selenium.chrome.ChromeDriver;
import org.openqa.selenium.Keys;
import org.openqa.selenium.interactions.Actions;
public class hkey
{
        public static void main(String[] args)
    {

    String baseUrl = "http://google.com/";

    System.setProperty("webdriver.chrome.driver","E:\\chromedriver.exe");
        WebDriver driver = new ChromeDriver();

    driver.navigate().to("http://www.google.com");
    driver.manage().window().maximize();
```

WebElement owe=driver.findElement(By.linkText("About"));

Actions oAction= new Actions(driver);
        oAction.moveToElement(owe);
        oAction.contextClick(owe).sendKeys(Keys.ARROW_DOWN).sendKeys(Keys.ENTER).
build().perform();

}
}

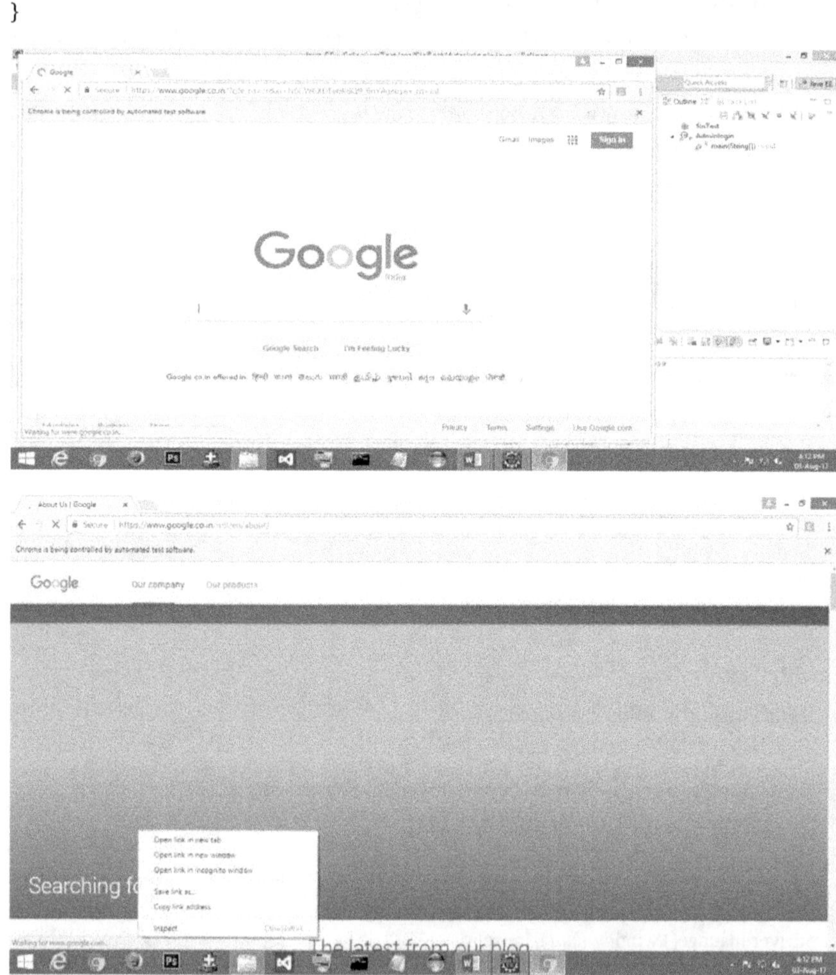